Pop Up
Business
FOR

DUMMIES®

Pop Up Business

FOR

DUMMIES®

by Dan Thompson

A John Wiley and Sons, Ltd, Publication

Pop Up Business For Dummies®
Published by:

John Wiley & Sons, Ltd
The Atrium
Southern Gate
Chichester
West Sussex
PO19 8SQ
England

www.wiley.com

For general information on our other products and services, please contact our Customer Care Department within the U.S. at 877-762-2974, outside the U.S. at (001) 317-572-3993, or fax 317-572-4002. For technical support, please visit www.wiley.com/techsupport.

For technical support, please visit www.wiley.com/techsupport.

A catalogue record for this book is available from the British Library.

ISBN: 978-1-118-44349-1 (pbk) ISBN: 978-1-118-44347-7 (ebk)

ISBN: 978-1-118-44346-0 (ebk) ISBN: 978-1-118-44348-4 (ebk)

Printed in Great Britain by TJ International Ltd, Padstow, Cornwall

Contents at a Glance

Table of Contents

Part II: Building on Your Pop Up Foundations 35

Chapter 3: Building Your Team 37

Chapter 9: Cooking Up a Media Storm for Your Pop Up 139

Part IV: Running Your Pop Up 153

Chapter 10: Designing and Kitting Out Your Space....155

Introduction

●●

*R*ight now, towns and cities are filling up with pop up shops, pop up cinemas, pop up restaurants, pop up parks and pop up allotments. It seems like everything's a pop up now, and nothing's permanent.

Of course, *pop up* has become a buzzword and is being applied to all sorts of things that aren't really pop ups at all. So to be clear, a pop up is any project tailor-made to a specific space, which opens for a defined period of time, with a clear start and end date. More importantly, pop ups do something different, unusual and interesting; they're not about the everyday way of doing things.

Pop ups have been around for a long time. We only have high streets because markets, the original pop ups, became permanent fixtures in town centres. And since the happenings and arts labs of the 1960s, seeing work by artists, actors and musicians in unlikely venues has become common practice.

So if it's so old and so common, why is the term 'pop up' everywhere right now, and why are people so interested?

People have realised that pop ups are a great way to do business. They're ideal if you want to test a new venture. They're perfect if you run a home-based business or sell on the Internet and want some extra exposure. They deliver magnificent results as part of a marketing or promotional campaign. And they help brands build real, lasting relationships with customers.

They're also far easier to do than ever before. People have moved to do their shopping online, at out-of-town centres where parking is easier and in supermarkets that stock everything. With more empty shops comes more opportunities to strike deals for short-term lets.

So pop ups meet the needs of a wide range of businesses, and the opportunities are there for people who want to take them. Pop ups are becoming normal, and part of the way businesses work.

But until now, nobody has provided a comprehensive guide to how to devise and deliver a pop up. It's been assumed that the people organising a pop up will muddle along, with a mix of skills in marketing, design, project management, retail and customer service. But pop up people need more than that; they need a specific way of working that embraces the temporary nature of what they're doing and is agile and adaptable. This book is for those pop up people.

About This Book

This book is about creating, planning and delivering a pop up. If you've never opened a pop up before, this book helps you focus, keep on track and avoid mistakes. I show you how to gather the right people to help you and how to make them into a team that works together. And I help you with the more complicated issues, such as the legal aspects of a pop up and how to find funding.

You can also use this book as a reference, for subsequent pop ups. You'll find it useful if you've already opened some pop ups and want to make the process a little easier. And if you're thinking of making a pop up into a permanent shop, you'll also find this book helpful as it covers some skills you need to make that transformation a success.

Beyond the loose definition I use in the previous section, this book doesn't define exactly what a pop up is, by the way. Think of 'pop up' as a set of skills that you can apply to lots of different types of activity that can take place in lots of different spaces. Be as creative with your project as you can.

Conventions Used in This Book

This book is a jargon-free zone, because nothing's complicated about pop ups. I avoid the technical terms used in business books, the arts world and in planning and regeneration circles and instead opt for using plain English. When I do introduce a new term, I *italicise* and define it.

The only jargon I can't avoid is the term *pop up*, of course! For this book, a pop up is any project in an empty shop or other empty space that is limited by time, with a clear start and end date. A pop up shop in a department store is not a pop up shop. A market is not a pop up market. Pop up shops are always temporary.

I use the word *business* throughout the book, to keep the writing concise; whenever I say business, I mean business, community group, social enterprise, arts organisation or even individual!

I also use the word *shop*, but I mean any space where you choose to pop up.

Foolish Assumptions

I assume that you want to start a pop up and have a good reason to do so. This book helps you by giving you lots of tips, tools and techniques to use.

I assume that a wide range of people will read this book, including:

- ✔ Small business owners
- ✔ Marketing staff in larger businesses
- ✔ Specialists in marketing
- ✔ Community organisations
- ✔ Arts groups, organisations and individual artists
- ✔ Self-employed people
- ✔ Local government employees

That's quite a diverse audience, with a range of different levels of experience, skill and understanding. So I've made the assumption that you'll use the bits of the book that are most suited to your level of experience and won't read it from start to finish.

I don't assume that you have any pop up experience. I aim to give you enough working knowledge of each area to make a pop up happen successfully.

Most importantly, I've assumed that you're the kind of person who wants to get stuck in, is willing to have a go and enjoys learning new skills. If that's you, you'll find this book is both a good starting point and a handy reference that you can keep coming back to as you pop up, again and again.

How This Book Is Organised

This book is divided into six parts, each covering a broad subject area.

Part 1: Planning to Pop Up

You need to lay good foundations before you can build a pop up, so in the first part, I look at what pop ups are all about and at how to carry out research to help you understand your pop up and the wider market it will operate in. I look at how to define your aims and objectives as you write a pop up plan and at how to create simple risk assessments to make sure that your pop up is safe.

Part 11: Building on Your Pop Up Foundations

The second part of the book is where popping up all starts to feel real, as I discuss building a team to make your plans come to life. I look at the practical help you can get alongside more strategic partners. I talk about local authorities and the role they have to play. I also offer networking tips and techniques to help you make friends and influence people.

In addition, I talk about how to develop budgets and where you can find funding. And I also walk you through finding and securing the types of spaces that may be suitable for your pop up.

Part 111: Filling Your Pop Up with People

As your pop up is taking shape, you need to think about how to fill it with the right kind of people. Part III looks at creating a strong brand that people will recognise. I also discuss the range of marketing materials you can produce and how to make sure that they're efficient and effective. Social media is the most efficient and effective tool available, so I talk about how to use it – and examine how to work with more traditional media, too.

Part IV: Running Your Pop Up

Part IV looks at the physical space, outside and inside. I offer you tips for fitting out your space and look at the techniques used to design and lay out shops. I then explore how you can staff that space, to make sure that it's effective for your business and inspiring, interesting and entertaining for your customers.

Part V: Looking to the Future

Your pop up isn't over as soon as the doors close. In Part V, I show you how to measure the impact of your pop up. I look at how success and failure can impact your wider business and the work of your partners. I also talk about how to make sure that your pop up comes to a good end and how to tidy up not only your shop but also your assets, without leaving any loose ends.

Part VI: The Part of Tens

Every *For Dummies* book has this bite-sized bit at the end, full of handy tips, tools and techniques. In this part, you find some inspirational things to do in your pop up and discover some very practical bits of equipment you'll need.

Icons Used in This Book

The small icons in the left margins of the book alert you to special information and highlight some key things you need to know. In this book, you find these icons:

The target highlights something that you can use to improve the planning, delivery and experience of your pop up.

If I give a real or occasionally hypothetical example that illustrates a point in the main text, you'll find this icon next to it.

This icon draws your attention to an important point to keep in mind as you apply the tips, tools and techniques you're learning.

This icon highlights where things could easily go wrong and is a sign of pitfalls and dangers ahead.

Where to Go from Here

You can read this book in many different ways, based on your own knowledge and experience, but also on the finer details of the individual pop up you're planning. However, it's worth starting with the table of contents and the parts pages inside the book that feature a cartoon and a short introduction.

If you're new to pop ups, start with Chapter 1, which explains what pop ups are and why they're useful. If you're more experienced and have a clear idea of what you want to do, open at Chapter 2 and start planning.

And if your pop up is already underway, use this book as a handy reference and check back with it at each stage of the process.

However you use this book, remember it's a reference you can keep coming back to and plan on reading each chapter more than once. The more of the book you read, the more you'll make sense of the approaches and techniques in other chapters.

While a successful pop up is about some very practical skills, tools and techniques, it's also about a certain way of working, which is loose, light and flexible. And those skills will be useful to other projects you work on, so take this book with you.

Part I
Planning to Pop Up

"Einstein over there miscalculated our start-up costs and we ran out of money before we could afford to open a 24-hour store."

In this part . . .

Whether you're baking a cake or decorating the front room, it's the end result you want and it's tempting to rush right in to the fun bits. But if you don't get the preparation right, the cake won't rise and the wallpaper will fall. So planning is an essential part of any project, and that's especially true for a pop up, which doesn't behave like a normal business.

In this part, I help you lay solid foundations before you open your pop up. First, I look at what exactly a pop up is and why you want to open one. Then I unpick the process and help you create a plan that's firm yet flexible, able to keep you going in the right direction yet still agile enough to cope with changing circumstances.

Chapter 1

Welcome to the World of Pop Ups

*T*ake a look around, and you see pop up cinemas and pop up cafes, pop up shops and pop up workspaces. And even those establishments that have been around a long time may suddenly have the word pop up in front of them. What's going on with this pop up phenomenon?

In this chapter, you discover what pop ups are and why they've become so popular.

Just What Is a Pop Up?

So what separates a *pop up* from other projects? To truly qualify as a pop up, a project should:

- ✔ Use an empty or under-used space.
- ✔ Be time-limited, with clear start and end dates.
- ✔ Not aim for permanence.
- ✔ Be designed for demountability and ease of removal.
- ✔ Have the potential to transfer to a different site.
- ✔ Be in some way exclusive, distinct or special.

Pop up in action

Adidas opened a series of pop up shops across Europe. They used empty shops and were based around a simple set of steel-framed furniture and freestanding lights, which employees could put up and take down in one day. The locations weren't announced to the public, but carefully chosen individuals were invited using social media sites. The secret stores only sold two styles of Adidas's most desirable shoes.

Pop ups have been around a long time, in one form or another; they're very much a movement that started with artists looking for temporary space to exhibit work, hold stage shows or create studio spaces. And good pop ups still need a bit of creativity.

Throughout the years, most major towns and cities have things happening that you could call a pop up. Take London. You could draw a line from Shakespeare's reuse of the old gatehouse of Blackfriars Monastery straight to Camden's Roundhouse, which was used in the 1960s for theatre and music happenings. In South London, Brixton Art Gallery ran from 1983 to 1988 in an old carpet showroom.

More recently, Space Makers worked in 20 empty shops in a market just around the corner. Many of these businesses started as pop ups, but have become more permanent over time.

Some very famous people started out this way. Tracey Emin ran a shop in Bethnal Green for six months, with fellow artist Sarah Lucas. Called 'The Shop', it sold a range of products they'd designed and manufactured, and the pop up led to Emin signing with a major art dealer.

While London has boasted high-profile pop ups, others have existed around the world and are part of the wider movement of reusing old buildings. Think of Andy Warhol's Factory in

New York, the Musée du Louvre in a former palace in Paris or the mass of buildings in Berlin used as cafes, art galleries and nightclubs.

More recently, pop up has gone from being something creative people do to being something mainstream. Re:START, a pop up shopping mall in Christchurch, New Zealand, came about after earthquakes destroyed existing shops, with the aim of starting the regeneration of the city.

Shopping centre owners Westfield now dedicate space to pop ups in all their centres worldwide, and they're used by luxury travel brand Kuoni, designer Cath Kidston and even BMW (to promote its Mini brand), for example.

A range of businesses you'll be familiar with already use pop up shops:

 ✔ Halloween shops

 ✔ Firework stores

 ✔ Christmas markets

Making the Pop Up Decision

Pop ups offer many benefits to lots of types of business. Although artists were the first to recognise the benefits of pop ups, all business sectors, from small and home-based businesses to global brands like Reebok and Disney, widely use them.

You should pop up if you:

 ✔ Don't want a high street shop all year round.

 ✔ Want to do something different.

 ✔ Have enough people who'll come to your shop.

 ✔ Want to test out your ideas before committing big resources to a project.

Comparing pop up shops with traditional premises

Taking on any commercial premises comes with certain responsibilities, so why choose a pop up over more traditional locations?

In both situations:

- ✔ **You must sign an agreement for a set period and commit to paying rent, rates and utilities for that time.** The agreement is between you and the landlord and gives you both rights and responsibilities in law.

- ✔ **You need to fit out the interior with equipment, furniture and fittings.** Any equipment you use needs to be to a good standard, well-maintained and, most importantly, safe.

- ✔ **You must staff the premises and manage those employees.** Your employees also have certain rights and responsibilities, so you need to be aware of the laws regarding the use of employees or volunteers.

Even if you expect to only employ part-timers they too have rights, perhaps more than you may expect. Ever since The Part-time Workers (Prevention of Less Favourable Treatment) Regulations 2000 was introduced in the UK, part-timers have progressively had their employment rights brought into line with those of full-time staff.

Check out Liz Barclay's *Small Business Employment Law For Dummies* to help keep you on the straight and narrow.

Obviously, a pop up shop reduces some costs by being a short-term let and open only for a short time (see Table 1-1). Other costs, such as furniture and fittings or marketing, may actually be higher because the cost isn't spread over a long period of time. Of course, this generalisation isn't necessarily the case, and you can find lots of creative ways around that problem.

Don't forget that any saving is offset by reduced sales income from a limited period of opening.

Table 1-1	Pop Ups Versus Traditional Shops
Pop Up Shop	*Traditional Shop*
Short-term tenancy, low or limited rent	Long-term lease; rent-free periods may be available but rent will rise
Business rates and utilities to pay	Business rates and utilities to pay
Temporary interior, furniture and fixtures	Full shop fit-out
Limited direct sales	Ongoing sales and regular customers
Fixed-term staff, high induction costs for short-time working	Permanent staff with regular responsibilities

Counting the advantages of pop ups

So why pop up at all? The answer is that pop ups aren't usually a straight rival to traditional retail; their goal is to do something different. More often than not, sales are only part of the reason for opening a pop up.

Essentially, pop ups are useful for business because they can:

- ✔ Provide a space for businesses that don't need year-round premises, for example, seasonal shops or online retailers.

- ✔ Offer a chance to test or prototype a new business model.

- ✔ Allow market research of a new product, range or service.

- ✔ Give a product, range or service an attention-grabbing launch or increase its profile.

- ✔ Reinforce an existing brand and its customer loyalty.

Online meets the real world

One special thing about pop ups is that they give online brands a space to meet the real world.

Do you have a copy of...?

Ministry of Found was a secondhand record shop, opened as part of a viral ad campaign for Yell. A much earlier campaign for Yell's predecessor, *Yellow Pages*, saw an old man phoning secondhand bookshops, enquiring about a book called *Fly Fishing* by J. R. Hartley. The sign-off was him giving his name to the bookshop owner who had a copy – J. R. Hartley.

This 1983 campaign was updated to mark Yell's move into digital, with a dance music DJ called Day V Lately trying to find a copy of his single, *Pulse and Thunder*. As part of the campaign, Yell opened a pop up shop in London, selling secondhand dance music. Day V Lately could be found in the store, as could his single. The pop up gave the TV campaign valuable media coverage and helped to spread the brand virally online.

Brands like eBay, Amazon, MySpace and Yell have used pop ups to market and promote their services so that they have a presence in the real world. These companies weren't focused on sales figures; they were all more interested in reinforcing their online presence and increasing their web sales.

At the other end of the scale, many tiny online sellers are using pop ups to increase their sales. People who sell from home are increasingly coming together with other traders to sell from a shop for a short period of time.

Doing Your Research

However great your pop up idea is, it's probably not innovative – it's almost certain that somebody has done it before you. Previous examples include pop up gardens and parks, pop up shopping malls and independent shops, pop up cinemas and theatre shows, pop up cafes and restaurants and pop ups that pretend to be real shops when they're actually just marketing stunts.

Reading up on past pop ups is an essential part of the process and can help you shape and refine your plans. Any plan is based on assumptions, and research helps you make good assumptions.

Research shows you some good ways to achieve your aims, helps you be realistic about what you can achieve and also stops you from repeating mistakes other people have made.

 Time spent on research isn't wasted; it means less time correcting mistakes in your plan further down the line. When a big company does something wrong, it has time, resources and finance to carry on. If your time, resources and finance are more limited, mistakes may mean the end of everything you've worked for.

Avoiding common mistakes

Here are five common mistakes (and how to fix them):

- ✔ **The wrong location:** Being off the high street, even if only a few metres away, can mean low footfall. Visit the location, watch and count how many passing customers you might get. Think about how to increase footfall while you're open.

- ✔ **The wrong look and feel:** Making your shop look cool is important, and it must match your brand and customers. Find the balance between bohemian and high-end retail and play with the temporary nature of what you're doing. Look at how successful retailers present their stores and take inspiration from their style.

- ✔ **The wrong opening hours:** Staffing your shop is the biggest commitment you'll make. Open at hours that match local traders and footfall patterns. Make it clear to visitors when you're open and when you're closed.

- ✔ **The wrong atmosphere:** Your shop needs to be welcoming without being overpowering and pushy. The right layout of furniture, fixtures and fittings and a clear brief for staff will help find the right balance. Again, look at the welcome you get in successful stores.

- ✔ **The wrong marketing:** You need to reach the right customers to match what you're doing. Too glossy and corporate can be off-putting if you're running a community project, and you can't be too scrappy if you're selling a high-end product like art.

Finding the information you need

Most people who've run pop ups are more than willing to talk and share their experiences. If you find a pop up shop that's similar to your idea, get in touch and ask for advice.

A number of websites are dedicated to the pop up phenomenon and are a great short cut to find out about pop ups past and present:

- ✔ www.emptyshopsnetwork.co.uk: Features regular write-ups of pop ups across the UK.

- ✔ www.londonpopups.com: A listing site for pop ups in the UK's capital, updated weekly.

- ✔ www.popupspaceblog.com: A look at pop ups and the issues surrounding them.

- ✔ http://popupcity.net: A blog about shops, mobile pop ups like food vans and other temporary projects.

The media have fallen in love with pop ups, and their articles often give valuable insights into what pop ups are really like and what they really achieve.

If you can't find anything in print, don't forget to do online research. Most projects pop up and then down again without any formal documentation or evidence they ever existed. However, in this social media age, everything leaves some legacy, often in the form of a blog, some short films or a page on a social networking site.

Of course, search engines are a good place to start finding those breadcrumbs. Commonly used phrases include: *Pop up shop*, *Pop up store*, *Pop up restaurant*, *Pop up*, *Temporary shop*, *Meanwhile*, *Meanwhile space* and *Meantime*.

You can also find up to the minute information using Twitter. Search for the hashtags #emptyshops, #popupshop and #popuppeople.

Try to use alternative search engines as well as Google – for example, type *pop up shop report* into Google and then into Bing, and you get very different results.

Asking for Help and Support

A number of organisations have been working with pop ups for a while, and they all try to provide help and support to people starting their own pop ups.

These organisations are all small with limited time and resources, so do make sure the answers aren't available elsewhere and that you know exactly what you want when you approach them:

- ✔ Check the organisation's website first to see whether the answers are available.

- ✔ Read any documents, such as reports or guides.

- ✔ If you can't find an answer, get in touch and be specific and clear about what you're asking.

Empty Shops Network

www.emptyshopsnetwork.co.uk

Set up by Revolutionary Arts, this project aims to freely share resources, provide example projects and act as a focus for finding new uses for high streets. You'll find good information here, as Revolutionary Arts has been running pop up projects in shops, churches and public spaces across the UK since 2000.

Renew Newcastle

http://renewnewcastle.org

This project aims to find artists, cultural projects and community groups to use and maintain empty buildings in the Australian city of Newcastle until they become commercially viable or are redeveloped. Renew Newcastle has inspired similar projects in other cities across the world, including Leefstand (see next section).

Leefstand

http://leefstand.wordpress.com

Renew Newcastle (see preceding section) is a direct inspiration for this project in the Netherlands, which has worked with a number of organisations in Rotterdam to create inspiring new uses for empty shops.

3Space

http://3space.org

With a portfolio across the UK, 3Space is effectively a letting agent for not-for-profit and charitable organisations. 3Space is developing resources to help people run pop ups.

The Meanwhile Project

www.meanwhile.org.uk

Led by the Locality (formerly the Development Trusts Association), The Meanwhile Project began as a UK government-funded response to the problem of empty shops. The Meanwhile Project works with landlords to save them money until more commercial tenants are found.

Chapter 2

Developing Your Pop Up Plan

....

....

*P*lanning a project is always a good way to spend your
time. Planning makes the whole project less tricky,
as you can see clearly who needs to do what, when. A plan
breaks a big pop up into bite-size pieces.

The process of writing a plan also helps you understand why
you're doing the project and the benefits it can bring to other
people.

In this chapter, I tell you everything you need to know (and
think about!) when writing a pop up plan.

Planning a Pop Up

A plan used to be a flat drawing on a piece of paper, such
as a sketch of a building or an industrial widget. A plan then
became broader and covered time as well as space. Planning
is looking into the future. Business plans try to nail every
possible alternative universe with data, market research and
detailed analysis.

But plans for pop ups are slightly different. They tend to be much faster, for one thing, but they also include lots of uncertain things.

US politician Donald Rumsfeld said:

> *There are known unknowns. That is to say, there are things that we know we don't know. But there are also unknown unknowns. There are things we don't know we don't know.*

Rumsfeld could have been talking about planning a pop up.

Writing Your Plan

Planning a project goes through many stages and is never really finished.

The best pop up plan is an adaptable working document that helps you by making sure you do the work you need to do. Having a clear plan also stops you getting distracted by things you don't need to do! It's not a set-in-stone definitive document that restricts you. Your plan should be short and simple enough that everyone involved in the pop up can read it, understand it and refer to it whenever they're uncertain.

Your plan should talk to an audience inside your business sector as well as possible partners outside of it, so avoid jargon and slang and use plain English. Author and journalist Peter Fryer wrote a book about how to write well called *Lucid, Vigorous and Brief* (Index Books) – the title is a good guide to writing, even if you don't read the book!

When writing a plan:

- ✔ Use simple English
- ✔ Be clear
- ✔ Excite people
- ✔ Keep it short

Although many people may have a passion for your project, it's best for one person to lead on the writing so that it conveys a coherent idea and a clear message. Of course, different areas of the plan may need expert input.

If one person in the organisation is responsible for the writing, that individual will also have enough of an overview to act as captain when needed – and can swing the biggest, most lumbering vessels around quickly when the wind changes direction.

Don't spend so long coming up with a plan that you're more involved with a plan than a pop up. Make your document adaptable and update it when your information changes. A business plan is a live document and always subject to change, not a set-in-stone list that you can't move away from.

Following the Agile Philosophy

The *Agile Methodology* started in software development, where it was used to describe a process that changed and adapted as software was built.

The simple idea behind the agile philosophy is that it's more important to get something up and running so that you can test and refine it with real people using it instead of planning it to the finest detail before launching it. If you plan for too long, you may be too late, you may be making something nobody actually wants or you may find that your competitors have got there first.

Key to the agile way of working is the idea of developing things that respond to the needs of people using it, rather than just the needs anticipated by the planners and designers.

Even a few years ago, software could be in development for years before being released with a big, thick manual to help users. Nowadays, it's common to see a website with the word *beta* on it, which means the product is an early release and is still being built and tested.

Agile in action

The agile philosophy is a style of working that you can apply to all sorts of disciplines. It's especially good for creating pop ups because pop ups are often planned and delivered in a short time and need a degree of flexibility.

Being agile also means that you can provide a service that feels much more tailored to your customers so they feel more valued.

The agile methodology is nothing clever, by the way. Every cafe is agile, serving the type of cake its customers want and brewing the blend of coffee that most of its customers want to drink!

To be agile:

- ✔ Aim to be up and running as early as possible.
- ✔ Welcome change.
- ✔ Get your team to work together daily throughout the project.
- ✔ Build projects around motivated individuals.
- ✔ Trust people to get the job done.
- ✔ Measure progress in actions, not words.
- ✔ Reflect on how to be better, and tune and adjust regularly.

Perfect for pop ups

An agile approach is perfect for pop ups because:

- ✔ **You may need to grasp an opportunity quickly** – for example, if a good location becomes available at short notice.
- ✔ **You may have to change your plans without much warning** – for example, if a long-term tenant rents a shop you were considering.
- ✔ **You may have to add new products** – for example, if supply of one you were planning to stock dries up.

Remember, though, that agile is still a form of business planning, and isn't an excuse for not planning! As the old business cliché has it, if you fail to plan, you plan to fail.

Defining Your Pop Up's Purpose

Your project needs a clear, defined purpose – an *aim*. Your aim must be clear enough to focus your activity and easy to explain to other people. In addition, you need to make sure that you either have or can find the people and the resources to meet your aim.

If you're adapting an agile way of working (see preceding section), a clear aim ensures that, as you respond to opportunity or change, you're still achieving what you set out to do.

Pop ups have all sorts of different aims, such as the following:

- ✔ Provide a space for a seasonal sale or event.

- ✔ Offer a chance to test or prototype a new business.

- ✔ Carry out market research for a new product, range or service.

- ✔ Provide an interesting way to launch a new product.

- ✔ Reach a different audience than the usual one.

- ✔ Occur in a different place to the location where you usually do business.

- ✔ Be a special event to increase customer loyalty.

- ✔ Show how your brand stands out from its competitors by doing something different.

Of course, a pop up may have several aims from the preceding list. For example, you may host a Christmas event for your most regular customers and use it to launch a new service.

No matter which aims you choose or how many you have, each aim must:

- ✔ Say clearly what your pop up will do.

- ✔ Be short, interesting and brief.

Identifying Milestones and Objectives

After you've defined an aim, you can start creating objectives. You start by identifying milestones and then coming up with objectives based on those milestones.

To transform your aim (see preceding section) into a realistic pop up plan, you can't beat pen and paper – you can create a rough, visual plan in a matter of minutes:

1. **Start by writing the aim of your pop up at the top of the page.**

2. **Draw a timeline down one side of the paper, starting with today's date and ending after your pop up closes.**

   Mark in the opening date and closing date.

3. **Sketch in key milestones leading up to the opening.**

   These milestones are called action points, and they help create a To Do list. You want these milestones to be practical, measurable, achievable and timetabled. Keep them as simple as possible.

4. **Sketch in milestones for after you close.**

Coming up with milestones

Milestones may be to recruit staff to your team, contact the media, source fixtures and fittings, get the keys to your location and so on. Of course, the exact milestones will vary depending on the nature of your pop up.

Don't worry about capturing every last detail now and don't consider how you'll reach those milestones just yet. Write next to each milestone the things you need to do to reach it – the actual steps to that milestone.

Milestones for after you close may include restoring the shop to the condition in which you found it, returning keys, completing any evaluation for funders and so on. Table 2-1 shows examples of actual milestones.

Table 2-1	A Timetable of Milestones	
Timeline	*Milestones*	*Steps*
1st March	Create plan	Write down aim, identify objectives, identify partners
7th March	Research potential locations	Decide on the shop
1st April	Recruit promotional team	Recruit graphic designer, web-site and social media team
13th April	Confirm location	Sign property agreement
16th April	Start marketing	Design and print leaflets and distribute press releases
30th April	Source shop fittings	Find furniture and display stands
14th May	Access shop and prepare it	Clean shop, decorate and put up signs
19th May	Prepare to open	Send out launch invites, invite VIP to open and recruit staff
28th May	Open	Enjoy!
11th June	Close shop	Clean shop, make repairs and remove signs
15th June	Return keys	

From this rough timetable and these milestones, you can develop your objectives.

Developing objectives

Objectives are specific steps to meet an aim and don't stand by themselves. They supply the details of what you must do and when you need to achieve that aim. Because objectives are specific and timetabled, you can identify when you've achieved an objective. And, of course, if you achieve all your objectives, you will achieve your aim!

In Table 2-1, each of the things you need to do is listed in the second column. These items are your objectives; you just need to fill in the details a little more.

For example, the milestone 'Source shop fittings' is too general and needs specifics to form an objective. Think about what you need. The objective may become 'Source 10 tables and 40 chairs, tablecloths, shop counter and equipment to serve tea and coffee, available from 14th May–14th June'.

After you identify all the objectives, you have a very effective To Do list and can start to make your pop up a reality.

Looking at Budget Basics

A *budget* is the total amount of money you have; a *financial plan* is how you'll spend it. I look at financial planning in Chapter 4 and at some of the ways you can raise the funds as well. A budget helps you make sure the funds you need are in place before you start.

Don't confuse budgets with financial plans, although the two go hand in hand.

Initial costs

Start with the initial expenses, the stuff you need to get the project up and running and get the doors open:

- Materials to do the shop up – paint and polyfilla, brushes and sandpaper.
- Furniture, fixtures and fittings.
- Electrical items, such as a kettle, vacuum cleaner and portable heaters.
- Printed publicity, such as leaflets, posters and business cards.
- Signs, window vinyls and graphics and an A-board pavement sign.
- A website domain and a website.
- Media advertising and leaflet distribution.
- Administration costs.

At this stage, it's a mix of making estimates and making enquiries. You need to know the rough size of the shop you hope to use and have a vague idea of the location as well.

Ongoing costs

You also have to add the stuff that your pop up will use after you're up and running and work out a weekly or monthly cost for these items:

- ✔ Business rates (more about these in Chapter 5).
- ✔ Utility bills (usually only electricity and water).
- ✔ Insurance coverage.
- ✔ Tea, coffee and biscuits for staff.
- ✔ Toilet paper and soap.
- ✔ Window cleaner and cloths.
- ✔ Mobile phone calls.
- ✔ Pay-as-you-go broadband, whether it's a mobile broadband 'dongle' or a WiFi router.
- ✔ Website hosting.
- ✔ Media advertising and leaflet distribution.
- ✔ Staffing.

Expect staff costs to be the highest percentage of your budget, and you probably need to spend at least 10 per cent of your total budget on marketing and publicity.

Your funding

After you estimate the rough figures for the cost of your pop up, you need to work out the potential income, either from sales or from other funding. This amount is your budget. A rough estimate of the costs – the money going out on bills, staffing, marketing and so on – tells you whether this budget is enough or whether you need to look at increasing it. Write up all the money that's coming in. This income may include:

✔ Funding or budget found within an organisation.

✔ Public donations.

✔ People paying contributions to the project, such as artists paying to hang work.

✔ Small amounts of sponsorship from local businesses, including donations of goods to support your project.

✔ Grant funding from local authorities, Arts Council England or from trusts and foundations.

✔ Income from sales.

Crunching the numbers

Always be realistic about what you can do with the resources you have and include options for different levels of resources and budget. Scrapping a project because you haven't secured the maximum amount of funding is a bit like throwing the baby out with the bathwater – if the project's really good, you'll find a way to make it happen.

Does your income exceed your initial and ongoing costs, that is, your total outgoings? If so, your pop up's in business!

If not, you need to look at either where you can save some money from your expenditure or increasing your income to match.

In some cases, you may have to accept that your pop up will lose you money. Your aims might make it worth losing money though, for example if you're delivering a community project or an experience for loyal customers.

Your income target

Now we come to the heart of your plan. How much do you have to sell if, as is very likely, your funding won't cover all your costs? Table 2-2 shows a sample income target plan.

Table 2-2	A Sample Income Target Plan			
Month	*1*	*2*	*3*	*4*
Costs				
Initial	1,000			
Ongoing	1,000	2,000	3,000	3,000
Total costs	2,000	2,000	3,000	3,000
Less funding				
Donations	300	300	300	400
Sponsorship	500	500	500	500
Contributions		100	200	300
Total funding	800	900	1,000	1,200
Total costs minus total funding = income you have to make from sales to stay afloat	1,200	1,100	2,000	1,800

If you think your pop up looks like needing a serious amount of money, take a look at *Understanding Business Accounting For Dummies,* by John A. Tracy and Colin Barrow (Wiley), from which this table is adapted. There you can find all you need to know about cash flow.

Managing Risks

As well as financial issues, you also need to consider other risks inherent in running a pop up. To do so, you can carry out a risk assessment.

Although a risk assessment sounds like a scary venture, you actually manage risks all day, every day, and on most days, you manage just fine. Get out of bed, don't trip, head to the kitchen (full of risks) but make a cup of tea and some hot toast without spills and burns, and so on. So don't worry about risk assessments, because they mean you don't have to worry so much about the risks themselves.

Managing a pop up's risks and the health and safety requirements largely comes down to common sense and being careful without being overly cautious.

You can do a risk assessment as you plan. In fact, looking at the broader issues during the planning process is a good idea. However, be ready to carry out a more detailed assessment when you have the keys to your premises.

Communicating the risks

After you assess the risks, make sure that you brief everybody working in your pop up about them and how you're managing them. You can convey this information through an informal induction as people come to the space for the first time – much the same as welcoming someone to your house and saying 'Mind the step as you come in'.

Keep a copy of the complete risk assessment in the shop, clearly labelled, for people to refer to if they want to. Be prepared to update this assessment if new risks are identified.

The Health and Safety Executive (HSE) provides lots of guidance, advice and even some useful templates to help you manage the risks in your workplace: www.hse.gov.uk/risk/fivesteps.htm.

Conducting a risk assessment

When you're assessing risk, you need to look at three areas:

- ✔ Fire safety
- ✔ Health and safety
- ✔ Security

The following sequence of questions makes risk assessment really easy:

1. **What is the hazard?**
2. **Who might be harmed?**
3. **How could that person be harmed?**
4. **How big a risk is it?**
5. **How can I minimise that risk?**

The simplest way to carry out a risk assessment is to create a five-column table and complete it during a site visit. Label each column as shown in Table 2-3.

Using your table:

1. **Walk around your pop up and look at what may cause harm.**
2. **Ask other people who'll be using your pop up what they think.**

    They may have noticed things that aren't immediately obvious to you.

3. **Consider whether you can eliminate the hazard altogether.**
4. **If you can't eliminate the hazard, think about how you can control the risks so that harm is unlikely.**

You don't have to be a health and safety expert to carry out a risk assessment, and the simpler it is, the easier it is for everyone to follow.

Table 2-3 shows a real example for a pop up event on Worthing Pier, which takes in some everyday risks alongside some unlikely ones.

Table 2-3	Risk Assessment			
Potential Hazard	**Who Is at Risk?**	**What Is the Risk?**	**Level of Risk**	**Risk Reduction**
Falling off pier	Individuals may fall off and into the sea	Fall from height Drowning	Medium	Assess slip, trip and fall hazards prior to the event Place railings around the sides of pier
Pier collapse	Everyone at the event	Panic as individuals are crushed or fall into the sea, sustaining related injuries	Low	Know Worthing Pier evacuation procedure Engineers to check structure monthly
Weather conditions	Everyone at the event	Strong winds, heavy rain, lightning strike, squalls and so on	Low	Postpone event if the weather conditions cause concern Cancel event if the conditions are unsuitable

When carrying out your risk assessment, remember to be clear about hazards and risks, and how to manage them:

✔ A *hazard* is anything that may cause harm – for example, an oddly placed step, a kettle full of hot water or a slippery floor.

✔ The *risk* is the realistic chance, high or low, that somebody may be harmed.

✔ Most important is how you'll manage that risk, which in most cases is easy and comes down to common sense.

Fire safety

The risk of fire in your pop up is probably quite low, and the main thing to consider is how to evacuate staff and customers from the premises quickly. Make sure that fire exits and routes to them are clear and well-marked. Agree with staff where to meet after an evacuation.

To minimise risk, make sure that anything not in use (for example, packaging or surplus stock) is stored safely and sensibly.

Tidy away rubbish and remove it from the premises daily. Most pop ups generate surprisingly little waste, particularly if you encourage staff to take their own rubbish home to recycle it.

Check out the UK government's useful guide: 'Fire Safety Risk Assessment – Offices and Shops' (`www.communities.gov.uk/publications/fire/firesafetyrisk2`).

Follow this fire safety checklist:

- ✔ Make sure that you have a phone available to make emergency calls.
- ✔ Clear away rubbish and safely store other materials and resources.
- ✔ Mark fire exits and ensure that routes to them are clear of obstructions.
- ✔ Test any alarms and equipment.
- ✔ Have an evacuation plan in place and make sure all staff and volunteers are aware of it.

Health and safety

Your risk assessment is a great help, but most accidents happen when people are careless or something goes wrong. Keeping your pop up neat and tidy minimises most risks and enables you to see quickly and clearly any that arise.

Carry out simple visual checks before you open your pop up every day and make sure that all staff are aware of potential risks and how to manage them. Remember to keep the staff briefing simple so that people don't get confused or unnecessarily worried!

In addition:

- Have a phone available to make emergency calls.
- Keep public areas clean, tidy and free of hazards, such as stacked boxes.
- Close and clearly mark areas not to be used by the public.
- Visually check electrics and any portable electrical items for damage, exposed wires or broken cables.
- Allow only responsible staff and volunteers to use any specialised equipment.

Security

Last but not least, you need to manage the security of your pop up and the people working in it. Again, common sense is the most important thing.

Here are a few tips to keep your pop up secure:

- Make sure that you have a secure or at least an inaccessible area to store personal goods, such as bags and coats, and encourage staff to use it.
- Set aside an area where stock or other unused goods are safe and secure and not open to the public.
- Ensure you can lock the property securely when not in use and don't store anything valuable where it may be stolen.
- Provide a phone for emergency calls.
- Close and lock doors and windows when premises aren't in use.

Part II

Building on Your Pop Up Foundations

©RICHTENNANT

SWIM WITH THE GIANT SQUID

SWIM WITH THE MORAY EELS

SWIM WITH THE JELLYFISH

SWIM WITH... S

SWIM WITH OCTOPI

"Since we lost the dolphins, business hasn't been quite the same."

In this part . . .

Running a pop up business is all about collaboration. No man is an island and you can't run a pop up alone! In this part I look at building a team, planning budgets, finding funding and how to charm the keys out of people so you can open your pop up.

Chapter 3

Building Your Team

'The first thing John Wayne always did was put together a posse,' says CJ Cregg in the TV show *The West Wing*. And now, that's what you've got to do. Your posse needs to have all the people in it who can make your pop up happen.

In this chapter, you discover how to assemble your team. You identify the practical day-to-day partners you need to help you open and run your pop up. You also see how to find strategic partners who'll help you achieve the bigger aims of your pop up. You also find out how to harness volunteers to your vision.

Recognising Why You Need a Posse If You Want to Succeed

It's great to have a leader at the front of your business, leading the charge and wearing the biggest stetson. After all, it's hard to think of Virgin without Sir Richard Branson, Amstrad without Lord Sugar, Ann Summers without Jacqueline Gold, or The Body Shop without the late, great Dame Anita Roddick. These great, visionary people are strongly identified with the brand they've built. However, it's the team behind these visionaries that makes it all come together, delivers an experience for customers and means the business can get bigger and survive in the rough and tumble of the wider world.

Building a team is difficult. In small organisations, delegating can be hard, and trusting people to get on with their tasks can be even harder. That's especially true if your pop up is a personal project, driven by your beliefs and by your own brand.

But a larger organisation doesn't mean you'll have an easier time assembling a team. In larger organisations, the challenge is to find the right people, get them enthused and also give them a sense of ownership of your pop up.

Always make your posse from people who can do things better than you can. Lots of people employ people who can't do the job better and then spend even more time trying to show them or, even worse, fixing their mistakes. Use your time for the things you do best; use your staff to do the things they can do better than you.

You face an extra challenge, too. In a pop up, it's less like building a team in a traditional business and more like putting together a team for a theatre production. For the curtain to rise on time in a pop up:

- ✔ You don't have a lot of time for the team to bond.
- ✔ You don't have time to test everybody's strengths and weaknesses.
- ✔ You don't have time to get to know the quirks of people's personalities.
- ✔ You have to work fast.
- ✔ You have to trust the team to make independent decisions.
- ✔ You have to be able to expect a level of professionalism.

So it's essential to get your posse together, make sure they all ride in the right direction and remember why they're a posse in the first place.

Figuring Out Your Staffing Needs

Before working out exactly what staff you need, you have to figure out when you need them and what they do. People can agree to work with you more easily if their roles are clearly defined. In addition, when they know what they're supposed to be doing, people will deliver far more!

Using your project's timetable, work out when you need staff to do what. (You can find more detail in Chapter 2 about creating a timetable.)

In terms of staff, consider your:

- ✔ **Management team:** Helps you make the planning decisions as you develop the project.

- ✔ **Marketing and communications team:** Works with both traditional and new media to ensure that your customers find your pop up.

- ✔ **Design team:** Makes decisions about branding alongside your marketing and communications team, as well as the layout and interior of your pop up alongside your maintenance team.

- ✔ **Maintenance team:** Handles practical jobs, such as decorating, fitting out and moving furniture.

- ✔ **Front-of-house team:** Staffs the shop when it's open.

In smaller pop ups, you'll probably find that a lot of those 'teams' are actually the same people. (I've worked on pop ups where most of the teams are me!) With your timetable, you can see the areas for which you may need to round up extra people for the posse.

The heaviest staffing will be immediately before and after your opening, but you'll need plenty of staff while you're open. Draw up a rota for the number of days you're open and break each day down into morning, lunch and afternoon shifts. Block in any special events, such as a launch party or evening opening. Look at shops near yours; do they have any early closing days? If so, you can close at these times, so mark out those sessions. You now have a clear idea of the time commitment while you're open.

Sharing for success

Buurt Flirt opened a pop up on Nieuwe Binnenwag, the longest shopping street in Rotterdam. The space was used to showcase work produced by local artists and designers, for community events and workshops, and also housed a small cafe. Buurt Flirt shared the space with meshprintclub, who set up a screenprinting studio in the back half of the shop. The shop itself was managed by Leefstand Co-Labs, set up to create partnership between people wanting to create pop ups. By working together, the partners were able to make maximum use of the space, share costs and involve more of the local community.

Finding People to Help Your Pop Up

Pop ups can fulfil lots of different functions, as you can see in Chapters 1 and 2. And that means lots of people, including those outside your business sector, are interested in making them successful.

Don't be afraid to ask people to help you with your pop up. When you're doing something worthwhile, people around you will want to get behind you and offer help. Many pop ups can happen only because people gather round, give extra help and go the extra mile, and that's no bad thing. However, in most cases, you should pay people.

Plenty of people will join your posse because of a direct benefit for them, such as selling their goods or raising the profile of an organisation they work for.

Some people, though, will be willing to volunteer time, materials or other support, either because your pop up has caught their imagination or because it offers some fringe benefit to them, such as learning new skills or pursuing a hobby. Use volunteers if you can, but look after them! (For more on using volunteers, see the 'Recruiting volunteers' section later in this chapter.)

Don't let partners distract you from the overall aim of your pop up. After you have a posse, if you're not careful, they'll all gallop merrily off in the wrong direction – at great speed and with great enthusiasm! Watch out for partners who start to bend your pop up to their aims, not yours.

In this section, I look at how to find the people you need to make your pop up not only a success, but also a bit easier for you.

Partnering with other crafters and businesses

The biggest problem for many pop ups is staffing; they're time consuming, both in the planning, fitting out and while you're open. Depending on what you plan to do, you may be able to share the time among a group of people.

For example, many crafters are using pop ups to sell their handmade products and share the opening times between all the makers involved.

Other pop ups provide more than one thing – a shop with a cafe, say. As a result, a number of people or even businesses can share the staffing responsibilities. If staffing is likely to be a problem (and being open 9 to 5 every day is a long time), think carefully about who you can share your pop up with.

Hiring staff

As well as finding partners, taking staff on for the period your pop up is open may well be worthwhile. Take on temporary staff who can do things better than you. For example, if customer service and direct sales aren't your strongpoint but are part of your pop up, take on staff who can handle this area.

You can use social networking websites, such as Facebook, Twitter and Linked In, to find and recruit staff. (Find out more about social networking in Chapter 8.)

Temporary staff options

Employing temporary staff means that both you and your staff have rights and responsibilities. UK employment law makes no difference between temporary and permanent staff, but various employment rights are based on workers being employed for a period of continuous service. Of course, a pop up may not fulfil this time-based requirement.

In the United States, the Internal Revenue Service (IRS) looks closely at companies that rely heavily on temporary staff. Companies may be required to pay tax on temporary workers if the IRS believes classifications are suspect.

As a pop up, you can use a *fixed-term contract*. This contract is between the employee and the business they work for; it is not used to employ staff through an agency. The contract must end on a particular date, which will probably be the closure of the pop up. A person on a fixed term contract has the same pay and benefits as a member of full-time staff.

Alternatively, you can use *freelancers*. A freelancer is self-employed and therefore responsible for her own tax and national insurance contributions. You must be careful, as you can't use freelancers just to avoid legal responsibilities.

You can check up on current legislation on employers' tax obligations with regard to freelancers on the HM Revenue and Customs website: www.hmrc.gov.uk/paye/employees/start-leave/special/freelance.htm.

For businesses in the US, check out the IRS website at: www.irs.gov and click on Business and then Employment Taxes.

Employed versus self-employed

Knowing the difference between employed and self-employed staff is important.

In the UK, staff are:

- ✔ **Employed:** They work for you and don't have the risks of running a business.

- ✔ **Self-employed:** They're in business on their own account and are responsible for the success or failure of that business.

In the US, the IRS determines staff status as employed or self-employed by carrying out three tests:

- ✔ **Behavioural:** Who controls what the worker does and how she does it?
- ✔ **Financial:** Are business aspects of the job, such as expenses, tools and suppliers, controlled by the payer?
- ✔ **Relationship:** Are there employee benefits and a long-term relationship?

Using local trades

Your posse is great, but some jobs always exist that are better done by somebody else.

Yes, you can handle Word and Photoshop – but would a good graphic designer make your pop up even more impressive, both to customers and other partners? (You can find out more about branding in Chapter 6, by the way.)

Of course, you can slap on a coat of paint to freshen up the space, but would a local decorator be able to help and do a neater job? Can a local carpenter help make repairs or tidy up the space?

Can a local shopfitting company help with the kit out? Or could a local furniture store loan you furniture for the short time your pop up is open, in return for advertising? (Chapter 10 has more details about designing and kitting out your space.)

Work through your timetable and look for points where the workload is particularly heavy. Subcontracting work may not save you money in these area, but it may save your sanity!

Try to source local trades for as many jobs as possible; one frequent criticism of pop ups is that they damage existing business by operating on a cheaper model. Offset that criticism by giving back to local trades where possible; doing so makes financial sense, and it's also a good way to spread word-of-mouth news about your pop up.

Finding strategic partners

While building a team for the practical, day-to-day running of your pop up is important, getting a gang of strategic partners behind your pop up will really increase your clout.

Write a list of everyone who supports, is affected by or is interested in your pop up but who won't be directly involved in either the fitting out or the day-to-day running of it – these are your *stakeholders*. Talk to other people, as they may think of others who you don't immediately think of.

 This stakeholder list needs to be a living document, and you update it regularly. Start writing your stakeholder list as soon as you start thinking about your project. As you discuss your pop up with more people, watch this list grow.

Stakeholders aren't automatically going to become partners in your pop up. You'll have to decide whether to invite stakeholders to become strategic partners. Of course, they may choose not to get more involved in your pop up even if you invite them.

Stakeholders are useful to your pop up because they can:

- ✔ Help you reach a wider or different audience.

- ✔ Access additional resources, such as staff or practical items like furniture.

- ✔ Have useful information to make your work easier, such as data about the local area.

- ✔ Give you additional support, such as training, advice or mentoring.

- ✔ Add credibility and authority to your pop up.

Coming up with a win-win situation

 You may risk compromising your pop up if you don't involve stakeholders, either as a strategic partner or just by keeping them informed:

✔ You may miss something important that your pop up could be doing.

✔ You may upset someone; if people feel ignored, insulted or just overlooked, they may oppose your pop up.

Think about how your pop up can help stakeholders by matching it to their plans and priorities:

✔ **Nearby business:** Will you increase footfall, which helps local shops? Does your pop up raise the profile of a place in the media or via social media? If so, your partners could be the Chamber of Commerce, Federation of Small Businesses, business networking groups and nearby shops. It's worth talking to these groups as early as possible.

✔ **Tourism:** Is your pop up going to be noticed outside the immediate area, perhaps generating national media stories? Will customers travel to your pop up? If so, consider working with your local council tourism department, a town or city centre management company and local media. After you have your plan in place, contact these people and explain how your pop up meets their needs.

✔ **Economic development:** Are you supporting local independent businesses? Are you using local suppliers? Are you creating new jobs? If so, your local council economic development or regeneration departments, Chamber of Commerce, Federation of Small Businesses and business networking groups will want to work with you.

✔ **Education and training:** Can you train local people? Could you involve a nearby school, maybe by talking to their business studies students? Is it possible to take on an intern or an apprentice? If so, schools, colleges, back-to-work schemes and training providers may be able to work with you.

✔ **Local voluntary and community groups:** Do you offer work for volunteers? Can you raise funds for a local charity while you're open? Will you be able to promote the work of a charity or not-for-profit organisation? Or can you raise the profile of an issue that's relevant to a charity or not-for-profit organisation? If so, you may be able to find partners who are charity or not-for-profit organisations; locally, you may be able to locate a forum for community and voluntary groups to help with your search.

✔ **Arts, culture and heritage organisations:** Does your pop up have space to display artwork? Will you use local creative industries, such as graphic designers or interior designers? Is your venue of interest because of its heritage? Artists, designers and arts groups can bring a lot to your pop up, but also consider civic trust and heritage groups. All these organisations tend to have good local networks as well.

Approaching potential stakeholders

After you have a list of stakeholders and have decided which ones to invite to become strategic partners, you need to approach them. A web search should turn up key contacts in the local council, schools and colleges and other organisations. But imagine walking up to a stranger in the street and asking them to help with your pop up; they're unlikely to get involved.

However, your network of friends and colleagues, past and present, can probably help. Instead of approaching a potential stakeholder cold, you can use both real-world and social networking to see whether you can find more direct contacts. (You can find out more about networking in the 'Making Friends and Influencing People' section later in this chapter, and Chapter 8 covers using social media in more detail.)

 To help approach possible partners, put together a one-page handout about your project; at this stage, you don't need all the details, but you do need to show the big idea. Use short text, written in plain English and not in jargon. Explain clearly why your pop up benefits the audience and users of the service you're sending it to, as an aid to making contact.

Drawing in friends in media and marketing

While Chapter 9 contains much more about bloggers and broadcast journalists, it's worth thinking about how you can get them even more involved in your pop up. In the modern media world, 'content is king', and certainly everyone involved in publishing – whether web- or paper-based, written word, film or audio – is looking for good content. Your pop up will provide a good story.

Strategic media partners can help you build awareness and excitement around your pop up. They usually offer a guaranteed amount of coverage in return for their branding being on your publicity and prominent in your pop up.

You shouldn't give away that kind of space unless it's for something really exceptional, but a good magazine, newspaper or blog that reaches your target customers is worth its weight in gold.

Could you persuade a local newspaper, radio station, blogger or podcaster to write up the whole of your pop up, from start to finish? Free tools help you do it yourself, but an established, trusted outlet has a wider audience, and your pop up can reach more people.

Be careful with media partners, as you may alienate other writers, broadcasters and bloggers if your pop up is too closely allied with their rivals! If journalists feel insulted, ignored or overlooked, they'll ignore your project, and you'll miss out on valuable exposure for your pop up.

Striking a deal with people who own property

If you can make the people who own property into strategic partners, you're onto something good. At best, you'll have regular access to spaces, help and support for your pop up.

Showing off business space

Pop ups help property owners showcase their available properties, possibly resulting in a lease. For example, Worthing Lions Club worked with the Empty Shops Network and secured the use of a former carpet showroom, owned by the local council. A pop up market and a programme of events, exhibitions and activities showcased 50 local charities. The event was supported by a £5,000 grant from the local council and attracted 12,000 visitors in six weeks. One visitor was the managing director of local software company, Fresh Egg. Inspired by the space he saw, his company took a lease on the building, spent half a million pounds refurbishing it and now have 85 staff working in offices there. Every month, the staff spend around £2,500 in local sandwich shops. The original pop up showed the space off and brought new use, delivering a measurable benefit to the landlord and to local business.

Pop ups deliver a number of benefits to the owners of empty properties. They:

- ✔ Repaint, refurbish and restore run-down property.
- ✔ Show off the space to possible new tenants.
- ✔ Support neighbouring shops and businesses.
- ✔ Can save landlords business rates.

Recruiting volunteers

If you're doing something interesting and it has some social, community or ethical benefits, you may be able to harness the power of volunteers. Volunteers provide an obvious benefit to your pop up, thanks to extra staff and more support. And, of course, any social, community or ethical benefits help your pop up get even more media profile.

But you can also deliver benefits to your volunteers. Perhaps you can help your volunteers:

- ✔ Learn or develop new skills.
- ✔ Feel more engaged in their community.
- ✔ Boost their job skills and consequently their career options.
- ✔ Meet a diverse range of people and improve their social skills.

For more about recruiting and working with volunteers, or to post an opportunity for volunteers, visit www.do-it.org.uk. For youth volunteers, go to www.vinspired.com.

For an informal way to get volunteers together for a particular job, such as cleaning up your shop, look at www.wewill gather.co.uk.

 Volunteers and employees are two different models of working, so do be careful not to confuse the two. If you treat volunteers the same way you do employees and use them to carry out something essential to your business, then you may have a legal duty to pay them. In several legal cases, volunteers have taken legal action against unfair dismissal or discrimination or requested the minimum wage for their activities.

Making Friends and Influencing People

To make sure that your pop up has the biggest impact, you need to make friends at every level.

Making friends gives you the chance to influence them and get them working for and acting as advocate for your pop up.

People tend to either love or hate networking, but making friends, from the playground onwards, is a form of networking. Often, the people who say they hate networking are the most natural networkers, and what they really hate are formal, official networking events, which can feel forced! In this section,

I use the phrase *networking* to cover both formal events and the kind of networking you do every day.

Not everybody that you talk to is going to love your pop up, so you need to understand the stance people take. If people object to your pop up, you need to hear why. And that means not just hearing, but working to understand. You may even want to make adjustments to your plans so that your opponents don't make trouble for your pop up.

Mastering successful networking

Networking has soft skills that make it an art, and hard skills that make it a science. This section looks at some hard and fast rules, as well as some more creative tips for successful networking.

The key to networking is being able to explain your idea – and Chapter 2 can help you be clear about the aim of your pop up and how to communicate that vision.

Successful networking involves three steps:

- ✔ **Introducing:** First, you need to make a clear introduction, both for yourself and the pop up as a whole. I cover that topic in more detail in the upcoming 'Delivering your elevator pitch' section.

- ✔ **Listening and remembering:** Listen carefully; listening is much more important than talking. Remember what you hear and find a way to file useful information away for future reference. Write brief notes on business cards as you collect them! Keep all business cards you collect in a box on your desk; you never know when someone will come in useful.

- ✔ **Following up:** Follow up any useful conversations with an email or tweet and follow up really useful discussions with a cup of coffee somewhere quiet.

Explaining the benefits

People buy something, whether it's a product, service or an idea, because it has some benefit for them. They're not interested in how clever it is, what the technology behind it does or why it's an innovative idea. You're probably not worried about the typeface or the binding techniques used for this book; you're interested in how this book can help you start a pop up.

To sell your pop up to people, think about the benefits to them.

Delivering your elevator pitch

An elevator pitch is a short, sharp summary of your project that captures the interest of people who may become partners, investors or even customers in your pop up. According to tradition, an elevator pitch should take under a minute – the time a lift takes to reach the top of the Empire State Building. Today, it's also worth getting your elevator pitch into a tweet – that is, under 140 characters.

So, what's the perfect pitch?

- ✔ Look at your pop up's aim (see Chapter 2). Condense that aim into short, sharp bullet points. Those points are the core of your pitch.

- ✔ A pitch shouldn't talk about what you do, but about what your pop up does for other people. For example, I don't say, 'I'm writing a reference book' but I do say, 'I'm writing something to help people who want to open a pop up'.

  If you want to deliver an elevator pitch about elevator pitches, you'll say something like, 'I help people tell other people really quickly what they do, to get the result they want'.

  Talking about the benefits of your pop up helps the person who's listening to relate to it and means they're more likely to buy in.

- ✔ Finish with a hook – a reason for the person you're pitching to to get involved in your pop up.

- ✔ Make your pitch in plain English, avoiding jargon and cliché, and ensure it sounds natural. Practise delivering it to family and friends, and watch and listen to how they react.

Keep your pitch short and sharp, make it easy to understand and add a hook.

Undertaking business networking

At business networking events, you can find people to help, others that are willing to point you in the right direction and strategic partners.

Business networking groups come in all shapes and sizes, and you can usually attend once or twice as a guest. These networking groups offer a broad range of businesses, and many groups deliberately allow only one business from each business sector. Other networking groups cater to one business sector, such as the creative industries. Finally, a number of groups for women in business tend to be very friendly and supportive. Even if you're a man, if your pop up offers benefits to women in business – for example, you're looking for local suppliers – do approach them.

Be prepared to attend networking meetings outside of normal business hours. Many groups meet early for breakfast or in the evening, after work. Practise your pitch before attending and have business cards or flyers to hand out with your contact details. If somebody gives you a business card, follow up with an email or a tweet later in the week.

More importantly, be prepared to listen and join in conversations; it may not be immediately obvious who you're going to want to work with in the future, so ask lots of open-ended questions and listen to answers. The best networkers listen more than they talk, in my experience!

BNI runs business networking events around the world. BNI meetings are all about referrals, and success is measured in the number of leads and introductions you can generate for other businesses who attend. Likemind takes a completely different approach with its groups across the globe. Meeting once a month, a Likemind meeting is a chance to drink coffee and meet 'likeminded people'. There's no agenda, but the meetings still help people to help each other. Many different networking groups exist. Try a few to find one you're comfortable with.

But remember, going to a group that has lots of people in your own business sector is pointless; you need to make new contacts! So you may need to step outside of your comfort zone occasionally.

Chambers of Commerce

Fifty-two Chambers of Commerce are accredited with the organisation British Chambers of Commerce, and many more organisations are unaccredited but still trustworthy! Membership of a Chamber is usually by annual subscription. Most offer regular networking, are keen to support new businesses and provide a good source for local expertise and experience.

Ask to attend a meeting as a guest before joining to see whether a Chamber will be right for your business, and use your visit to network.

To find accredited Chambers of Commerce in the UK, go to www.britishchambers.org.uk.

Federation of Small Businesses

With more than 200,000 members, the Federation of Small Businesses (FSB) is a lobbying group for the sector. It also provides a range of member benefits, including legal advice, guidance on health and safety, free banking and downloadable legal documents. With nearly 200 local branches, the FSB offers plenty of local networking opportunities so that you always have access to good local knowledge.

For more information or to join the FSB, visit www.fsb.org.uk.

Both the Chamber of Commerce and the FSB are well-known organisations, so some partners view membership as giving your business credibility.

Thinking big

While most people find it easy to think local, if your pop up is really good, you may be able to punch above your weight. Always think big!

Pop ups are being used for lots of different purposes, and it's recognised that they:

- ✔ Are entrepreneurial, at a time when the global economy needs new enterprise.
- ✔ Provide local solutions to bigger problems.
- ✔ Prototype and test new ideas for businesses, products and services.

All these traits can appeal to an audience of thinkers, strategists and writers beyond the local. Can you add national stakeholders to your list, and how can you engage them in your work – either directly or to provide research, evaluation and further understanding of your pop up?

Working with Local Authorities

Local authorities provide the step between local services and national policies. They also deliver a wide range of local services, collecting everything from rubbish to local taxes, which you need to consider as part of your pop up.

Local authorities will certainly be a stakeholder, but in this section, I look at the ways and means of making them more than that and discuss how you can include them in your list of strategic partners.

Understanding your local authority

People think of their local council as one body, with a big plan and a lot of power. The reality is quite different; a local authority is made up of lots of different departments, all with roles and responsibilities that overlap (and not always in the most obvious ways).

As in any large organisation, people are jostling for territory and power as well. To top it all off, *council officers*, who are often experts in their particular field, are led by *council members*, the people's elected representatives who might not be so expert in the field they're in charge of!

As if that's not enough, many parts of the UK have three levels of local council: parish, village or town; borough or district; and a county council on top.

In the US, each state has at least two layers of local government: counties and municipalities. Some counties are divided into townships. And municipalities can be split into authorities at city, town, borough and village level.

In both the UK and US, every level of local authority can have its own plans and priorities for a place, independently of each other.

Finally, regional plans or the priorities of national government can over-ride those local plans and decisions.

So it's less a question of 'understanding your local authority' and more an issue of 'understanding your many local authorities'! Identifying your stakeholders (see the 'Finding People to Help Your Pop Up' section earlier in this chapter) will help you work out which officers in which authorities you can work with.

Finding friendly officers

Council officers (the people paid to work for the local authority) are always keen to find ways to deliver benefits to local people for less work and less money. However, they also have to defend the roles and responsibilities of their departments, making sure that things happen that meet the targets in the plans they're working to. And they have to ensure that legal responsibilities are met. At the end of the day, though, their job is to help you to do things – not to stop you.

The best way to find out what local authority officers want is to ask them! Request copies of the strategic plans they're working to deliver.

Consider how you can work with officers who help to deliver:

- ✔ Arts, culture and heritage.
- ✔ Economic development and new business support.
- ✔ Tourism.

✔ Training, skills and education.

✔ Managing council property portfolios.

The more stakeholders you have in your many local authorities, the more resources you can unlock to help you.

Chapter 4

Funding Your Project

. . . .

. . . .

*P*op up, sell lots and retire rich; you could write that as your financial plan, but it's a bit rough around the edges and may not work out the way you intended!

Finding funding and managing the financial plan for your pop up is really important, but it's not like normal business accounting. Pop ups do something different, and in this chapter, I cover why it's often hard to see how to balance the books.

Remembering Your Aim

When you create a budget and a financial plan for your pop up, you need to remember what your aim is. With your aim in mind, you can be realistic about the amount you spend and on which areas of your financial plan. You can also be realistic about whether you're going to make a profit from the shop's income – or whether the shop's other purposes are worth the financial risk.

Many pop ups are about something more than sales. If your pop up is about any of the items on this list, then it's unlikely that sales will be the principal measure of your success:

- ✔ Offers a chance to test or prototype a new business model.

- ✔ Allows market research of a new product, range or service.

- ✔ Gives a product, range or service an attention-grabbing launch or increases its profile.

- ✔ Reinforces an existing online brand.

- ✔ Is about community engagement.

In these cases, look carefully at your budget. You may need raise it from funds for marketing, community engagement, research and development (R&D) or corporate social responsibility.

Be realistic about any targets you set in your financial plan. While you can carefully cost your expenditure, it's a little bit harder to estimate income from sales. Setting sales targets is only worthwhile if you have a good idea of your current customers and a reasonable expectation that they will visit your pop up.

Developing a Financial Plan

Don't confuse budgets with financial plans, although the two do go hand in hand. A *budget* is the total amount of money you have (see Chapter 2). A *financial plan* determines how you'll spend that budget.

Always be realistic about what you can do with the resources at hand. In your financial plan, include options for different levels of resources and budget.

Never scrap a pop up because you haven't secured the maximum amount of funding you thought you'd need. Pop ups are about being creative with limited resources; if all pop ups had the biggest budgets, they'd all be shops in city centres! If your pop up's really good, you'll find a way to make it happen, and some of the most eye-catching, innovative and talked about pop ups have happened on tiny budgets.

Calculating Your Income

To calculate your total income, you need to look at all the funding you raise to make your pop up happen and at any money you make while the pop up is open.

If your pop up has a bigger aim than just sales, it may be funded from budgets used for marketing, community engagement, R&D or corporate social responsibility. In a smaller business, you can probably make the decision to allocate such funds yourself, but in a larger business, you'll need to negotiate with partners in other departments.

Estimating your sales

Estimating what you may sell directly from your pop up, particularly if you're selling a new product or in a new geographical area, can be tricky.

Predicting sales is even harder if you're launching a new product or testing a new business idea. In this case, you don't know your customers, and they don't know you yet, as lots of sales are based on brand loyalty.

If you have past experience from events such as pop ups or markets you've run before, this can inform your sales estimates.

Without this information, you can only provide a best guess, based on the number of customers you expect to get. Testing the market in this way is a good thing for your pop up to do!

Your pop up may well start relationships with new customers or increase the loyalty to your brand that current customers feel. Some of your sales may be from customers you meet at your pop up, but who don't decide to buy until long after your pop up has closed. This situation is particularly true if you're selling high value items. I once sold a painting a whole year after somebody had seen it in a pop up gallery!

Testing the market

Second Gear was a pop up that opened in Margate, a seaside town in Kent that has been identified as having the most empty shops in the UK. The owner chose this location for the pop up precisely because he didn't know any customers locally; he wanted to test the market before committing to a full business plan and taking a longer lease. Selling 'lost and found men's clothing', the Second Gear pop up was able to prove that Margate didn't have enough customers to support a vintage clothing store for men. So by not selling enough, and providing evidence that such a business wouldn't work, the pop up was a successful test and saved the owner launching a business that would fail!

When you're looking at possible sales from your pop up:

- ✔ Be realistic about any sales targets you set.
- ✔ Think about ways to measure follow-up sales.
- ✔ Use the pop up to test the market.

Include your estimated sales in your income figures; you may want to include figures for high and low sales.

Look at how you'd cope in the worst-case scenario. A large business may be able to take a risk, but if you're a smaller business, you may be risking everything you've worked for.

Do create some mechanism for tracking any indirect sales that the pop up generates. It may generate good sales leads for you to follow up. Alternatively, you may see a rise in online sales as a result of the buzz created around your pop up. And finally, you may get customers who return sometime later to purchase something they saw in your pop up. These are harder to measure, of course, but may be a valuable source of sales!

Looking at other income sources

In addition to funds from sales and from other business budgets, you may also generate income from:

- ✔ People paying contributions to the project, such as artists who pay to hang work or other businesses sharing your space.

- ✔ Small amounts of sponsorship from local businesses, including donations of goods to support your project.

- ✔ Grant funding from central government, local authorities, Arts Council England or from trusts and foundations (see the section 'Finding Grants and Funding', later in this chapter).

Calculating Your Total Expenditure

To calculate your total expenditure, add up your:

- ✔ Start-up costs
- ✔ Ongoing costs
- ✔ Staff costs
- ✔ Bills, such as electricity and business rates
- ✔ Insurance costs

Add in some extra as a contingency against unexpected costs – at least 10 per cent of the total. You should now have a worryingly big figure, but don't worry. Looking at your income reveals how your pop up can work. (See the 'Calculating Your Income' section, earlier in this chapter.)

Start-up costs

To create a realistic financial plan, you need to start with a list of everything you're going to need for your pop up. Think about the big spends, such as fixtures and fittings, right down to the smallest details, such as tea bags.

Keep this list as a live document and refer back to it, updating it throughout the time you're planning and then delivering your pop up.

These lists may well include items you already have in stock. If you do pop ups regularly, you'll find some items get used over and over again – in which case you don't need to include them as costs.

You also may be able to borrow some items. For example, you probably don't need to buy a vacuum cleaner or a kettle, as you can borrow them from home for a short time.

I don't include staff costs in this list. If you're working in a larger business, consider the staff time that is allocated to this project. If you're in a smaller business or working alone, think carefully about the time spent on your project. (You can find out more about staffing your pop up in Chapter 3.)

Create a headline for the areas you need to spend money on and break them down into more detailed lists. Then add a cost to each item:

✔ Materials to do the shop up

- Paint

- Brushes

- Sandpaper, filler and so on

- Timber and so on for repairs

✔ Furniture, fixtures and fittings

- Tables

- Chairs

- Display stands

- Counter

✔ Electrical items

- Kettle

- Vacuum cleaner

- Portable heaters or fans

✔ Print and marketing

- Leaflets
- Posters
- Business cards
- Marketing or public relations company

✔ Branding

- Graphic design
- Signs
- Window vinyls and graphics
- A-board
- Give-aways and branded items

✔ Online

- Website domain
- Website creation

Work through that list carefully and identify any areas where you can save. Perhaps you can borrow furniture, fixtures or fittings or just use free websites such as Facebook and Tumblr instead of paying somebody to build a new website.

Ongoing costs

In addition to your start-up costs, you need to think about ongoing costs, which are spread across the time you're open. For a really short pop up (and some open for just a day or a weekend), ongoing costs will be like start-up costs; you'll have a big hit at the beginning of your project.

If your pop up is open for longer, you can spread your ongoing costs across that time. For many pop ups, these costs stay roughly the same; for example, if you buy a roll of ten rubbish sacks, it'll probably last for a month-long pop up. Of course, for a longer pop up, some costs, such as utility bills and business rates, will be higher too.

Here are some ongoing costs to keep in mind:

- ✔ Bills
    - Rent, even if a 'peppercorn' or token rent
    - Business rates
    - Electricity
    - Water
    - Gas
    - Insurance coverage
- ✔ Consumables
    - Tea, coffee and biscuits for staff
    - Toilet paper and soap
    - Window cleaner and cloths
    - Rubbish sacks
    - Computer peripherals – paper, printer cartridges and so on
    - Stationery
- ✔ Communications
    - Mobile phone calls
    - Pay-as-you-go broadband, a dongle or a WiFi router
    - Website hosting
    - Media advertising
    - Ongoing leaflet distribution

Again, work through the preceding list to identify any place where you can make a saving – for example, you may decide not to use leaflets and instead market your pop up online.

Utility supplies

In the shops most pop ups use, water and electricity are still connected, as the landlord and letting agents need to use them. If they are, ask the landlord or their agent to keep a reading and charge you for what you use – this arrangement is much easier than transferring accounts for a short period of time. (You can find out more about how this setup works in Chapter 5.)

If you're using a more unusual space or a shop where the utilities aren't connected, you may have to factor in reconnection costs.

Be aware: The contract may require a minimum time to run, so you may have to keep paying after you've left the space.

For short projects, using mobile phones and mobile broadband is easier than setting up a phone line and connecting broadband. You can use a dongle for individual laptops. A mobile WiFi router lets you run up to five laptops and should be adequate for all but the largest projects.

Insurance coverage

For a pop up shop, you need:

- ✔ Contents coverage
- ✔ Public liability insurance
- ✔ Employers' liability insurance
- ✔ Buildings insurance

Don't worry; you can usually cover all these items in one insurance policy, which makes coverage less complicated than it sounds.

Most major insurers offer packages tailored to the needs of small businesses and shops, which are very affordable. You can often set them up with a phone call or online. You need to know the space you're planning to use before enquiring, as insurance prices vary according to the shop's floorspace, its location and any security equipment fitted, such as shutters and alarms.

For a pop up, the building's landlord probably has the buildings insured already. This insurance covers the owner against damage to the building from disasters, such as fire and flood.

In some cases, such as when you're working with a local authority or within a shopping centre or market, the landlord may be able to offer you a more comprehensive insurance package for a small fee.

If not, consider taking out insurance coverage for your pop up. Your first port-of-call should be whoever provides your existing business insurance. Your current policy will have a number of items covered, depending on what your business does and the coverage you negotiated with the company. So your current insurer may already cover you for a pop up; it's not unusual, after all, for businesses to pop up at a trade fair or other event. If not, the company should be able to extend your current coverage.

As well as the major insurers, some people are offering specific insurance for pop up shops:

- ✔ **Pop Up Space,** a company supporting people running pop ups: www.popupspace.com/index.jsp?nav=insurance

- ✔ **Hencilla Canworth,** an independent insurance intermediary, with special knowledge of creative industries and temporary cover: www.hencilla.co.uk/default.aspx

All insurance is about managing the risks, and the best idea is to ensure that you don't need to claim anything. Take a common sense approach to safety by watching out for hazards and making sure that everyone involved in your pop up is aware of those hazards. (You can find out much more about how to identify and manage the risks in your pop up in Chapter 2.)

If you're working for a larger business or organisation, you need to verify that your company's insurance will cover your pop up shop or have alternative coverage in place. Talk to whoever is responsible and at all times make sure that you keep within any guidelines you're given.

Business rates

You're liable for government taxes on any profit from your pop up and should take advice from your accountant or accounts department if you're concerned.

But whether you make a profit or not, you're liable for some taxes and must ensure that you have the funds to cover these costs whatever happens.

UK

If you're occupying a building in the UK that's not a domestic property, you need to pay non-domestic rates (NDR), which are usually called *business rates*. (Chapter 5 covers business rates in more detail.) Business rates are a central government tax, paid by anyone operating a business from commercial premises such as shops, offices and factories.

How much you pay in business rates depends on:

- ✔ The rateable value of the property, which is set by the Valuation Office Agency.

- ✔ What multiplier central government sets.

- ✔ What rate relief schemes you're eligible for and which ones your local council applies when it works out your bill.

 Different schemes support businesses by offering reductions and business rate relief in England, Wales, Scotland and Northern Ireland. Check with your local authority for more details. Also check the government's Business Link website for up-to-date information: www.businesslink.gov.uk.

Local authorities in the UK have discretion to grant rate relief of up to 100 per cent to not-for-profit activity. Charities and amateur sports groups get a mandatory 80 per cent relief, which a local authority can make up to 100 per cent. Contact your local authority for more information.

United States

In the United States, each state has at least two layers of local government: counties and municipalities. Some counties are divided into townships, and municipalities can be split into authorities at city, town, borough and village level. All those entities can demand different property taxes.

The landlord is responsible for paying those taxes; you should be clear with the landlord about any business taxes you are liable for.

Staff

Staffing is one of the biggest costs for your pop up, and it's not something you can cut without impacting your opening hours.

Chapter 3 covers how to work out the staff you need in more detail. You need to include the total cost of all staff in your financial plan:

- ✔ For those employed by your business, the cost of the hours they'll spend planning and delivering your pop up.

- ✔ For subcontractors and freelancers, you'll probably agree to a set cost to deliver an agreed outcome.

- ✔ For temporary staff, the total number of hours will define the cost.

If you're using volunteers to help support your pop up, you must pay them reasonable expenses, such as travel. Volunteers shouldn't replace key staff without whom your pop up can't run, and you must manage and care for volunteers.

Finding Grants and Funding

Grants are subsidies, given for specific activities, often after an application process. The person who gets the grant must use it for the purposes specified in the application.

While the perception is that only charities can receive grants, that's not the case. Generally, grants are given to support the activity, not the organisation behind the activity, so they can be given to:

- ✔ Support research and development.

- ✔ Further charitable or community aims.

- ✔ Support a particular type of business.

- ✔ Help businesses increase their scale.

- ✔ Provide opportunities, such as training.

✔ Regenerate a particular neighbourhood.

✔ Support economic development in a particular location.

Applying for funding

You can apply for funds if your pop up does things such as:

✔ Provides training for young people.

✔ Helps regenerate a run-down street.

✔ Restores a historic shopfront or building.

✔ Drives footfall to support local traders.

✔ Engages with a hard-to-reach community.

Those are just some of the cases where pop up shops have received grants to support and develop their activity.

Not all funds will match the project you're planning, but you'll be surprised at how many diverse sources of funding are available. Make sure to apply for funds that are suitable and work closely with funders whenever possible. When you're working with funders, you'll have to work to a set time, provide a planned activity and usually monitor certain outcomes.

Locating funding

Funding for pop up projects is relatively new, so not many dedicated funds are available yet. However, the UK government has given grants to town centres to aid failing high streets in 2009, 2010 and again in 2012, so limited funds do exist and could support pop ups.

In addition, funding for arts-based pop ups is well established, so the UK's Arts Council may support pop ups.

You need to look carefully at what you're doing and how it can be funded from established sources. If you're working in a large organisation, you may have a funding officer who can help with this process. If you're a smaller business or organisation and have some community-minded aims, your local authority may have a funding officer who can help you.

Be careful that the search, draw down and management of funds for a pop up doesn't outweigh the need for funds. In other words, don't spend £1,000 of time to get a grant for £500! Also be cautious that the needs of funders don't change the nature of the pop up itself. Don't make finding funds the most important thing and don't waste time chasing funds when finance may not be the barrier to getting the pop up going.

Local funding

Local authorities may have limited funds to support local pop ups. In addition, some trusts and foundations support very local activity; for example, the Co-operative Membership Community Fund supports small, local projects across the UK.

National funding

National funding in the UK comes in three main types:

- ✔ **Public,** such as Arts Council England and Nesta. Public funds tend to come ultimately from central government and are raised by taxation. These funds are typically used to create economic outcomes, such as new jobs created, land redeveloped or new businesses started. Those from arts sources want to see audiences developed or new artworks created.

  These funds are never simple to draw down and generally require quite rigorous administration and accounting. Smaller pop ups should consider looking for this sort of funding only as a last resort, especially while public funding is being reduced.

- ✔ **Lottery,** such as the Heritage Lottery Fund. Lottery funds have clear, open and quite transparent application processes. Applicants can find plenty of guidance, advice and support. These funds are widely used for community projects of all sizes.

- ✔ **Trusts and foundations,** such as Jerwood Charitable Foundation. Trusts and foundations are charities that give grants to support their own aims and objectives. They have a greater degree of independence about who and what they fund, but are often small organisations so they may not even acknowledge applications.

For all pop ups looking for national funding, visit the Funding Central website at www.fundingcentral.org.uk.

Keeping the Books

Every business, however small or short term, has to keep track of income and expenditure. In the first place you need to know whether you're covering your costs, making a profit or about to lose your shirt. In addition, you have to produce at the very least a three-line set of accounts (income, less expenses = profit) to report your profit (or loss) to HM Revenue and Customs.

Bookkeeping is the name given to the way that you record all your transactions – paying the rent, buying in stock, taking cash in from customers and so forth. You could just shove all your bills and receipts in a box and try to unravel them later. But it's more practical and useful to have a system for entering transactions as you go along.

You can pick up paper-based books of accounts in stationers but as you can buy basic bookkeeping software systems for as little as £30 it usually makes sense to go down that route. You can get help in choosing software from Accounting Software Reviews (www.accounting-software-review.topten reviews.com).

Alternatively, if you really can't face doing the books yourself, you could employ the services of a bookkeeper. Professional associations, such as the International Association of Bookkeepers (IAB, www.iab.org.uk) and the Institute of Certified Bookkeepers (www.bookkeepers.org.uk), offer free matching services to help small businesses find a book-keeper to suit their particular needs. Expect to pay upwards of £20 an hour for their services. The big plus here is that professional bookkeepers have their own software.

You have to give the tax authorities a record of your trading activities. You can use the three-line account, which is a simpler way of providing details about your income and expenses, if your annual turnover is below the VAT registration threshold – £73,000 for the 2011–12 tax year (www.hmrc.gov.uk/factsheet/three-line-account.pdf).

Take a look at *Understanding Business Accounting For Dummies*, by John A. Tracy and Colin Barrow, to find out everything you need to know about keeping track of your finances and staying on the right side of the taxman.

Chapter 5

Finding Your Space and Your Landlord

Many towns, cities and villages are full of suitable spaces for a pop up. An American-style yard sale, a traditional English village fête, an old-style spiv selling from a suitcase and a temporary shop selling fireworks in the autumn can all be considered to be pop ups, and they're established, almost traditional models. But you can find far more interesting and exciting spaces to use. Where you hold a pop up is entirely up to you, and the only limit on what space you use is your own imagination.

This chapter looks at how to identify spaces, find out who can let you use a space you like and cope with not getting the place you set your heart on. I also cover the legal side of finding a space so that you can make sure you can secure the deal.

Being an Explorer: Finding Interesting Spaces

The perfect space for your pop up increases customer interest, brings the media along and ensures that the pop up is talked about after it's closed.

To find the perfect place for your pop up, you have to do some footwork and visit potential locations. But the first step in finding a pop up actually takes place before you set a foot outside. The following questions help determine the places you look at so that you're not running around on a wild goose chase:

- ✔ **Does a local space particularly match your pop up?** Sometimes, a building or public space seems ideal for a project. For example, Shakespeare's *Twelfth Night* features a shipwreck, so Rainbow Shakespeare thought Worthing beach would be a perfect stage set. The film *Brief Encounter* is set in a railway station cafe, so for the On Location Film Festival, the local station's waiting room was the perfect place for a pop up cinema screening. Or to go even further, Damian Cruden staged his Olivier award-winning production of the *The Railway Children* in an empty railway station with a real steam train.

- ✔ **Where would your pop up have the biggest visual impact?** Sometimes you want your pop up to scream your brand from the rooftops – maybe literally. Part of the The Beatles' legend is built on staging their last performance on the roof of the Apple headquarters – a legendary pop up concert! To celebrate Barbie's birthday, Mattel chose the very ordinary terraces of Ash Street, Salford, but painted them bright pink. Look for places where your pop up can stand out, grab the attention of passers-by, get media attention and be remembered.

- ✔ **Does a pop up put your brand right in front of your target audience?** If you're selling to a target audience, put your pop up right where it will be. During every London Fashion Week, top designers fill expensive spaces. The London Fashion Bus pulls up outside the venue, and the converted Routemaster red bus gives young designers an opportunity to be seen. The Energy Cafe pops up from a converted horsebox and serves food found within a few miles of its temporary location. Maybe the guy selling coffee from the Piaggio van outside the station is the pop up king.

✔ **If your pop up has an ethical angle, does a venue match it?** Lots of pop ups are about more than just selling, and many highlight a particular issue or debate. Scottish food writer and cook Christopher Trotter wanted to celebrate his nation's seafood and highlight issues of using only local food, so he opened a pop up restaurant in a small fishing village. Finding the right venue helps make the point.

Empty shops

Towns are full of empty shops, but don't think they're all immediately available. Some may be held by companies that have gone into administration so they can't be let, while others may be under negotiation with future tenants. And in some cases, the landlord is happy to let these shops sit empty as they're just an asset on a balance sheet! Look out for shops with 'To Let' signs as they're ready to use. If shops don't have a sign up, you can search the Land Registry (in the UK), but even this isn't guaranteed to find the landlord as it may tell you no more than the name of the company that owns the building.

Shops owned by your local council are also good to target. Contact your council's commercial property department and ask for a list of all the properties it manages, not just the ones currently vacant. The complete list will include unlikely properties, such as warehouses, kiosks and so on, that may suit your purpose but that the council may not be advertising commercially.

Be prepared to understand the different needs of landlords, their agents and local authorities. (See the 'Charming the Keys Out of People' section later in this chapter for more on this.)

Whatever you're after, look for shops off the beaten track; wander down side streets, find unused corner shops in the middle of a neighbourhood and look at smaller parades of shops outside town centres.

Look at empty shops in shopping centres and markets. As these are usually under the control of a centre or market manager, you only have one person to negotiate with.

Spend a day doing some street research. Use a printed street plan and coloured stickers to map empty shops in your area, and you'll soon see patterns emerge. Or get a group together to spend a day mapping your town centre and create a crowd-sourced survey of the area. *Crowdsourcing* means asking lots of people to contribute information, and it's often used these days as a way to find funding.

Blog, film and take photos as you explore. The Empty Shops Network uses social networking site Flickr to collect photos of empty shops, so add them to that (www.flickr.com/groups/emptyshops).

Open shops

You can find plenty of open shops with spare space inside them. While department stores are the obvious example, as they let spaces or concessions to brands all the time, look at places like local cafes, pubs and photographic studios, too. They often have lots of floor space, and perhaps your pop up could fit in a corner of their shop.

UK department store chain John Lewis enables charities, health and arts groups to use the spare rooms in its many stores. Nineteen branches across the country have made rooms available for opera groups to rehearse, cancer support groups to meet and theatre companies to practise.

You can also find a business with a whole empty room – the back room of a pub, for example, or an unused store room upstairs, or an empty outbuilding.

Shopping centres and markets may have space you can use outside their normal units, in-between existing shops in a square, plaza or central space.

Find an existing shop or cafe that compliments your brand and work together. Build a friendship with a local business owner, and you may potentially have a regular space to pop up. And your pop up, with lots of media coverage and a buzz on social media, brings extra customers to their shop, too.

You can take collaboration further and follow a trend for *hybrid retail* – shops that do more than one thing, such as a bookshop and cafe combined, or a record shop that's also a gig venue. Your pop up may lead to a full-time hybrid business. Some suggest that, in the future, everything will be a coffee shop . . . and certainly, a coffee machine in your pop up shop is a good way to encourage people to linger!

Community spaces

Towns and cities are full of useful spaces, run by and for the community. Look at all the buildings used locally for workshops, classes and meetings, from the church to the town hall and the community centre to the railway station.

Community centres tend to let their spaces by the hour, so they may be a more expensive option. However, you may be able to negotiate a deal, particularly on one of their less used rooms. Can you offer to help with marketing, redecorate a room or find volunteers for a job that the community centre needs doing in return for access to its space?

Other spaces may need some negotiation, particularly if they're not spaces that are usually used – but I've seen great markets in a local church and a cinema in the waiting room at a station, so it can be done!

Putting your pop up in a community building is easier than negotiating another space such as an empty shop. It means that you have some resources, such as tables and chairs, on hand. Also, the building has its own regular users so you have some ready-made customers. You could use a community space to test your idea and build a list of customers before going it alone.

To help you find community spaces, a number of websites let you search maps online. You can also add venues to these sites, even if you don't use them this time round:

- ✔ **Spare Place:** A crowdsourced map of rooms and other spaces that are available (started in the UK but available for use worldwide): www.spareplace.com

- ✔ **The Place Station:** Matching community assets, such as the local library, with people who can use them: www.theplacestation.org.uk

Council spaces

Your local council may own property for all sorts of reasons, and it's sometimes surprising what it does own.

Contact the council's property department for a full list, but look around you, too. The town hall, sports centres, theatres and public squares are the obvious ones.

But what about old works department buildings, light industrial units, stores, sheds, kiosks and shops? Most councils own a wide variety of unused buildings that may be suitable for a pop up.

Council property departments are tasked with finding a commercial rent for buildings they own, but you can still negotiate as they benefit from letting you use an empty building. You can tidy up the property, maintain it, cover the cost of heat and lighting and make the space look better for possible future tenants.

You can even show new tenants how good the building is. Council officers are accustomed to working on the basis of evidence, so give them examples of successful pop ups and clearly explain the benefits to them. Use the examples given throughout this book!

Regeneration, tourism and economic development officers in the local council have different agendas. Can your pop up help them in their work? Does your pop up help regenerate a rundown area, attract out-of-town visitors or incubate a new local business? If it helps these officials, get them on your side and see whether they can help you negotiate with the property department, too.

For Dummies . . . on the road

The *For Dummies* marketing team kitted out an old library bus to tour round the UK's town centres in 2011. The publisher took the authors of many of their books to different places, and ran workshops covering everything from playing the ukulele to keeping chickens. The tour gave customers a high-quality experience and an introduction to the many *For Dummies* titles available. More importantly, it reinforced the brand's identity as a good place to start learning new things.

Unlikely venues

What's the wildest, wackiest and most unusual way you could pop up? Think about exactly what space you need – and work out the minimum requirements, the absolute basics to make your pop up happen. Then start looking for unlikely venues that match your brand image and ideas. Can you pop up somewhere really unusual and create an experience that your customers love and talk about?

The more unlikely the venue, the more it will be talked about – both on social networks and by the media. And that's good for you!

Choosing a Space

Matching your pop up to a perfect place is both an art and a science. If you have a well-defined aim (see Chapter 2), you'll be able to find the perfect venue. Start by asking the following questions:

- ✔ **What size space do I need?** If you're selling a small range of products (or even a range of small products!), your space could be tiny. If you're selling furniture, you need somewhere bigger.

- ✔ **How far will my customers come?** If you're relying on lots of sales to total strangers, you need a high street space with good passing footfall. If you're offering something different or that's exclusive to loyal customers, they'll still come to you even if you're off the beaten track.

✔ **Is the footfall high enough?** You need a space with sufficient people passing, known as *footfall*, to meet your aim, whether that's selling to customers or meeting people in the local community.

Charming the Keys Out of People

Spotting a space you like is easy enough, but finding out who owns the space and then winning them over to let you use it can be harder. The key to success is to start early and to network. If you're reading this book, you're well on the way to opening a pop up, so now's the time to start networking.

Networking isn't something you do once a week at a breakfast meeting. It's something you can do all the time.

Getting a meeting

You're asking the person who owns the property to do you a favour by giving you a short let probably at low cost. Would you ask a complete stranger for a favour? Probably not. Would you ask a friend or colleague? Of course you would! So the key to charming the keys out of people is to get to know them first and then ask for the favour later.

Find places where you can make friends with the people you need to meet. Your local Chamber of Commerce probably runs regular meetings, for example, and you should be able to attend once or twice as a guest before you have to sign up.

Most towns have a variety of business networking groups, and again, most let you attend once or twice as a guest to get a feel for the group. Use search engines to find local groups, or ask the business or economic development team at your local council for a list.

Be prepared to attend with a short, clear and punchy explanation of what you do and have business cards or flyers to hand out with your contact details.

Pitching your proposal

Staying lucid, vigorous and brief (see Chapter 2) is especially important for pitching your pop up to other people. You need to be able to explain your idea easily and in simple terms – the 'lucid' bit. You need to do it with some energy – be 'vigorous'. And as you're dealing with busy people, the 'brief' bit explains itself.

Write down your pitch initially. Start by explaining your pop up. Say exactly what it is you do and don't use any jargon that's specific to your business sector. Add some sizzle and tell people why your project is special. Explain why it's a pop up and not a normal shop.

When you're writing your pitch, think carefully about why other people would want to help you. You need to find something in it for them, whether they're a neighbouring shopkeeper, a local councillor or a letting agent. Think about including those benefits in tailored versions of your pitch.

Your pop up pitch needs to end with a *call to action* – a firm end that results in something happening. The easiest is 'Can I have your email address and send you some details?' but you can be more creative.

Use as few words as possible and try out your pitch on family and friends. You want to be able to say it naturally, without sounding forced and rehearsed, and with enough energy and excitement to get people interested.

Some words are used a lot but don't mean anything – in fact, they usually hide what you're really talking about! Avoid clichés like you'd avoid the plague, don't go near jargon and never use words like 'exciting' and 'unique' in your pitch. *The Banned List* by John Rentoul (Elliott & Thompson) is a good guide to over-used words and phrases to avoid.

Preparing for chance encounters

Of course, there's really no such thing as a chance encounter – only putting yourself in the right place for the things that seem like chance to happen. Making sure that you're in the right place and ready to take advantage of opportunities is a really good pop up skill.

While you're planning your pop up, go to as many events where you might meet people as possible. Village fêtes, school fairs, charity fundraisers and civic functions are all places where you might meet somebody useful. Make sure that you have your pitch ready and can adapt the tone of it to different audiences. Carry business cards everywhere.

Losing a place

Securing a space for a pop up isn't always easy because you're asking for a short occupancy and probably offering a low rent and that puts you at the bottom of the letting food chain. Be prepared to lose a space you've been looking at because a better tenant comes along.

If you've built a friendly relationship with a letting agent and you lose a space, he'll probably help you find alternative premises. But make it easier for yourself in any case by creating an agile project that can change in response to circumstances. Don't be downhearted if you have to move somewhere different at short notice – that's all part of the fun of a pop up! (For more on being agile, see Chapter 2.)

The kind of places where pop ups happen, especially empty shops, are harder to book in advance. If you're paying a low rent and have a temporary tenancy, be prepared to be bounced out of the way if a more permanent tenant comes along. So try not to plan your whole project around just one space. Be agile and able to change direction if you need to.

Staying Legal: Leases and Licences

Although you're using a space only for a short time, you still have legal responsibilities. An agreement between you and the person owning or managing the space ensures no disagreements occur further down the line and cover you in case of problems.

Knowing what to include

Any agreement needs to cover:

- ✔ Who the agreement is between.
- ✔ What space it applies to and what you can use that space for.
- ✔ What changes you can make to the space (for example, with regards to redecorating or putting up signs).
- ✔ In what condition the property must be returned.
- ✔ The dates and times the space is to be used.
- ✔ Any costs, including rent or hire costs as well as utility bills, insurance fees and business rates.
- ✔ Who's responsible for what (for example, insurance, rubbish clearance and security).
- ✔ How to change or cancel the agreement.

Looking at agreement types

If you're renting a space, you need some type of agreement:

- ✔ **Hire agreement:** At the most basic level, if you're hiring a space, you should have a hire agreement. This is an agreement to borrow a space for a short period, and is used by places such as hotels and community centres to rent rooms.

✔ **Licence to occupy:** This is a step up from a hire agreement and is often used for temporary use of a shop. Technically, a licence to occupy means that a business can occupy part of somebody else's property for a set period of time.

✔ **Full lease:** This is a more complex legal agreement between two parties: the landlord and the tenant. Entering into a lease means you have legal responsibilities, so you should be very clear about what you're signing.

Whether you use a hire agreement, a licence or a lease depends on the length of time you want the space for, but also on the landlord. Some people are used to hiring a space, while others are more familiar with a licence to occupy for short-term tenants. A lease is typically only used for a longer period of occupation.

Checking out a hire agreement

A hire agreement is used when you're borrowing a defined space for a short period of time. It's the kind of thing you'd expect when renting a room in a community centre, hotel or other building that lets rooms by the hour, half-day or at a daily rate. A hire agreement enables the user non-exclusive use of an agreed area, for a set time, at a defined cost.

Using a licence to occupy

A licence to occupy is often used for the temporary use of space, so it's ideal for a pop up. The landlord and his agents still have the right to occupy the space as well – to show new tenants around, for example. And the landlord is still responsible for the maintenance of the structure of the building, so this type of agreement involves slightly fewer responsibilities, on both sides, than a lease.

When a licence to occupy comes to an end, the tenant must leave or negotiate a new licence; you don't have any automatic rights to remain in the property.

Looking at leases

A lease is usually for a set period of time, typically between 3 and 25 years. However, the UK government has commissioned a *meanwhile lease* to encourage temporary use of empty shops, which you can use for a pop up. This enables land-lords and tenants to sign a full lease, with various rights and responsibilities, for much shorter periods of time.

Seek legal advice before signing a new lease or taking over an existing one. Leases are often written in legal terms and can be difficult to understand.

A lease includes lots of detail, covering both parties and their rights and responsibilities, and uses the following legal jargon:

- ✔ **Landlord:** The property's owner.
- ✔ **Tenant:** You, the person who's occupying the property.
- ✔ **Property:** The exact location, often shown on a plan.
- ✔ **Lease period:** Usually a fixed period, but the lease may roll on from period to period, in which case this is explained.
- ✔ **Use allowed:** What you can use the property for.
- ✔ **Rent:** A weekly, monthly or annual amount.
- ✔ **Rent start date:** The date from which rent must be paid.

A lease also sets out your responsibility for any maintenance and repairs to the building.

Under the Landlord and Tenant Act 1954 (Part 2), you have the right to renew your lease at the end of the agreement, except under certain circumstances – when you've signed for a fixed period of six months or less, waived your rights when you signed or broken the lease in some way.

Paying Business Rates

If you're occupying a building that's not domestic, you need to pay non-domestic rates (NDR), which are usually called business rates. This central government tax is charged based on values set by the Valuation Office Agency. However, the administration is handled by the local authority, which means that your local council has little control over the charges, relief or support it can offer on them.

Business rates apply to shops, offices, pubs, warehouses and factories. But some entities don't have to pay business rates, including:

- ✔ Places of public religious worship.
- ✔ Most farmland and farm buildings.
- ✔ Public parks.

How much you pay depends on:

- ✔ The rateable value of the property, which is set by the Valuation Office Agency.
- ✔ The multiplier set by central government.

  The *multiplier* is used by your local authority when calculating your business rates bill. It indicates the percentage, or pence in the pound, of the rateable value that you pay in business rates.

- ✔ The rate relief schemes you're eligible for and which ones your local council applies when it works out your bill.

England, Wales, Scotland and Northern Ireland have different business rate schemes, and in all areas, the government offers different schemes and incentives at different times to support business. Do check with your local authority for more detail and check the government's Business Link website for up-to-date information about current schemes: www.business link.gov.uk.

If you're operating as a business, you're entitled to small business rate relief if you occupy only one property and its rateable value is less than £12,000. If you occupy a property with a rateable value below £18,000 (£25,500 in London), you're eligible to have your bill calculated using the small business multiplier. This relief is on a sliding scale and can be up to 100 per cent of business rates.

A small shop has a rateable value of £10,000. The current multiplier in that area is 41.3p. Therefore the business rates liability totals £4,130, but you're entitled to 50 per cent small business rate relief. So the bill sent by the local council is £2,065 for one year.

Local authorities have discretion to grant rate relief of up to 100 per cent for not-for-profit activity. Charities and amateur sports groups get a mandatory 80 per cent relief, which a local authority can make up to 100 per cent. Contact your local authority for more information.

All empty properties are exempt from paying business rates for three months after they become vacant. Certain types of property and properties under a set rateable value have additional exemptions. After three months, shops are eligible for 100 per cent business rates. And, of course, once shops are in use, they're eligible for 100 per cent business rates.

Part III

Filling Your Pop Up with People

The 5th Wave   By Rich Tennant

"Don't worry Mr. Brennen. The 'OPEN' sign is on the door. I can see it from here."

In this part . . .

Getting a shop open is easy enough; but as you can see from the empty shops in towns and cities, closing one is pretty easy too. Businesses fail for one reason, and that is that they haven't pulled in enough customers. Pop ups often don't need many customers, as they're targeted at very specific markets, but even if your target is low, you still need to reach it.

In this part, I look at all the different marketing channels that you can use, and which ones will work the best for your pop up. I start by helping you to create a strong brand, and then look at how you can spread that brand and the message behind it in different ways, from social media like Twitter to more traditional outlets such as local newspapers.

Chapter 6

Making an Impression: Branding and Marketing

*B*randing and marketing are big business now, and plenty of companies can help you at every stage of the process.

You may choose to outsource your branding to one agency, your day-to-day graphic design to another, your social media to one person and your PR work to somebody else entirely. Or you may decide to do it all yourself, perhaps with the help of a handful of friends and colleagues.

In this chapter, I help you make informed decisions, which-ever way you choose to do the work.

This chapter looks at creating a brand for your pop up. I assume that you're creating a separate, distinct brand just for this pop up. However, you could use this chapter to create a brand for a whole business.

Making Your Pop Up Brand and Marketing Distinct

However you approach them, all branding and marketing must contribute to the overall aim of your pop up. They must make it sparkle and shine, but they also need to be honest about what you're doing. If your marketing is just hype or it oversells a simple pop up, your customers may be disappointed.

A brand is bigger than simply creating a logo and a strapline. Branding tells people what a business stands for, what it does and something about the experience it offers.

Branding is developed over time and through various channels, such as:

✔ Consistent messages in adverts.

✔ Word of mouth buzz.

✔ Experiences using the business products or services.

Branding is the glue that holds all these messages and experiences together, helps the customer to recognise the business and differentiates it from others in the marketplace.

Extending your existing corporate brand

Ministry of Found was a secondhand record shop created as part of a viral advertising campaign for Yell, the online version of *Yellow Pages*. The shop opened as a Dance Music Exchange on London's Brick Lane for one week. During the week, '90s dance music stars made appearances, and the shop hosted a variety of events, workshops and a celebrity-filled launch party.

Ministry of Found had its own branding, with a logo and shop fit out that made it look like a real record shop. However, the Yell logo was applied to banners, signs and promotional items. The colour yellow was used on walls, in lighting and on the header cards in racks of records, which reinforced Yell's brand identity. Ministry of Found was designed and executed by marketing agency Shine Communications, with other elements of the larger campaign handled by other companies.

Keep your branding and marketing:

- ✔ **Clear:** Use it to say what you do in the simplest terms.
- ✔ **Consistent:** Apply the same elements to everything you do.
- ✔ **Coherent:** Tell the same story across lots of different channels.

A pop up brand is distinct and used only for a pop up project. However, your pop up brand may be an extension or development of an existing corporate brand – for example, as part of a marketing campaign or to test a new product or service. In this case, refer to any existing corporate branding guidance before reading this chapter.

Pinpointing Your Audience

The starting point of creating your brand is exactly the same starting point as your pop up – what's your aim? And your aim is nothing without an audience!

While looking at your branding, you have to start making some informed decisions about your audience.

I look at market research in more depth in the 'Mastering Marketing' section later in this chapter. Market research helps you refine your branding and marketing, but you need to have some idea of who your audience is before you can work on creating your branding.

Hopefully, you have some idea of who your customers are, perhaps because you've carried out market research prior to designing the branding for your pop up or you've got a business that's up and running so you know something about your customers.

Write down every group who might make up the audience for your pop up. Think about:

- ✔ Current customers.
- ✔ People you'd like to become customers.
- ✔ A wider audience who'll just be interested visitors.

Are these broad categories, or are they small sectors of society? Are you looking at a mass market or a niche market? Although a niche market has fewer customers, you can probably reach it more easily with tailored marketing, and you may ultimately be more successful in business, too. In a mass market, you're competing with big businesses that can afford to offer discounts and other incentives.

After you have an idea of your audience, collect together other things which you think already appeal to the people you've identified, such as packaging, website pages, magazines, images and advertising. Use this knowledge to inform decisions you make about your branding. You want to make sure that your pop up sits well in the marketplace occupied by other competing brands.

Give some thought to the people you *don't* want as customers as well. The hardest lesson for any small business is that some customers do exist who you just don't want. Thinking you must please everybody, all the time – 'the customer is always right' is all too easy. However, bad customers are out there. These bad customers don't have the money to buy the product or service you offer at the price you need to charge, or they require lots of hand-holding. Either way, they can become a drain on your company. Your branding can help you attract the right customers, while helping to turn away the bad ones.

Creating a Brand

A brand is about more than just a logo; it's the whole package that tells people what your company does and, more importantly, what it stands for. Your brand is an important part of communicating your message. It also represents your reputation. And your brand makes you stand out from the crowd.

Think about popular brands and how they create an emotional message:

- ✔ Coca-Cola is about youth, energy and fun but has a strong heritage and tradition, which suggests it's always been part of (and perhaps even the fuel for) youth culture. The brand isn't just a logo; it's the colour red, the shape of a Coca-Cola bottle and that distinctive white flash.

✔ Body Shop is about being clean and green. It's a campaigning brand that's interested in the environment, ethics and ecology. Body Shop has a memorable logo, which suggests Art Nouveau style but also looks like arms wrapping around something. Wicker baskets, plain cardboard and rough, recycled paper add to the eco feel in the company's stores.

Those examples illustrate that a brand is made up of a number of elements, including:

✔ **Name:** Your name says what your pop up is and hints at what it does.

✔ **Logo:** A graphic device you can use in all your marketing and in your shop design.

✔ **Strapline:** A short line that tells people more about your brand (think of Nike's 'Just Do It').

✔ **Style:** A set of fonts, standard colours and a defined way of applying these and the three elements above to what you do.

While this chapter looks at how you can create a brand, you'll probably want to work with a *graphic designer* to create logos and refine the overall look and feel. I talk more about working with graphic designers in Chapter 7.

Name

To paraphrase the poet T.S. Eliot, 'The Naming of Brands is a difficult matter/ It isn't just one of your holiday games'! Brand names need to be different but recognisable, unusual but memorable and hint at what you do without being obvious.

You can spend lots of money on a name. *Yellow Pages* became Yell when it went online, and more recently, the company paid Landor Associates a six-figure sum to create the new name 'hibu'. It's probably better that you work out your branding for yourself, to be honest!

We Are Bedford

We Are Bedford started as a year-long project to bring life to the town's empty shops. The project was started by two people who met on Facebook and was supported by funding from the RSA (Royal Society for the Arts). We Are Bedford staged a number of events in different places.

The Castle Quays Weekender was a two-day festival of pop ups, with shops, music venues and art galleries filling empty shops. A busking festival, with pop up stages across the town, and some drawing events in empty shops followed later in the year. To end the year, a Pop Up Emporium for Christmas sold work by local artists and makers.

Because the project kept moving from one place and project to another, strong branding with a powerful logo was important in building recognition and keeping an audience engaged. This branding needed to be flexible, adaptable and affordable as well.

Bonfire Creative Intelligence designed the We Are Bedford branding, which featured a cut-out like a rectangular paper doily and a cut-out, custom-made font. These branding elements could be used in a variety of different colours and formats.

The branding was used online and in a wide variety of printed materials. It was also applied to window vinyls, used to make laser-cut wooden signs and made up as a rubber stamp to apply to hanging tags and paper bags. Distinctive and eye-catching, the branding was applied consistently across many projects and soon built a loyal following for We Are Bedford.

Naming is more art than science, but some tricks help you come up with a name that works. Your pop up must have a name that:

- Sets it apart from competitors.
- Is memorable.
- Is easy for anybody to say, spell and pronounce.
- Suggests what happens inside.
- Sounds positive and upbeat.

✔ Is short enough to use in simple messages, such as when you tweet.

✔ Is better than 'hibu'!

If you're naming a pop up that's a project within a bigger business, consider whether you can give it a name that relates to that larger business.

I struggle every time I have to name a project, but these steps seem to work:

1. Start with your aim.

2. Create a list of actions; the things you'll do.

3. Look for associated language and phrases, particularly ones that are emotional or evocative.

4. Create combinations of the words you've written down until you find something that fits.

5. Test a number of names on friends and colleagues.

You can also use brainstorming to come up with a name, but in a focused way. In Table 6-1, I use as an example a pop up flea market. All the possible names are real ones, by the way, used by pop ups in the UK.

Table 6-1	Brainstorming for a Brand Name		
Aim	*Action*	*Associations*	*Possible names*
Market selling secondhand goods for local traders	pop up, shop, store, market, boutique, store, recycle, upcycle, remake, reuse	retro, vintage, secondhand, flea market, antiques	The UpMarket, ReStore, Second Gear

Ideally, you want complete ownership of your name because you need to use it across social media platforms and register good domain names such as .com. Check out `http://namechk.com/` to see if the name you're considering is available.

If your project is local, you may be able to find a name that's been used some distance away, but which local people won't be aware of. Or you may be able to add a place name; dozens of projects called 'Artspace' exist across the UK, but because they're called 'Coventry Artspace' and 'Artspace Portsmouth' that's not a problem.

Logo

A logo isn't a random mark; it's the cornerstone of your branding and should become recognisable, like the famous Nike Swoosh, the McDonald's golden arches or the Adidas stripes.

A good logo is:

- ✔ Bold and simple.
- ✔ Classic and timeless.
- ✔ Adaptable and flexible.

When you next go shopping, look for logos on packaging and ask yourself the following questions:

- ✔ Which logos leap out at you, and why?
- ✔ Which logos are serious and carry authority, and which ones are lightweight and humorous? What makes them different?
- ✔ Which logos suggest the brand is about things that are natural, organic or ecofriendly?

Swoosh!

Discussing logo design without a reference to Nike's famous logo, the Swoosh, is almost impossible. The Swoosh is a distinct shape, at once very modern and completely classical – it's often compared to the wing of the Greek goddess of victory, which the company took its name from. It certainly suggests movement and energy, which is ideal for a sports brand. It's simple and works well in a single colour. It can be applied to lots of different things, but wherever it is and whatever the size, it's instantly recognisable. The Swoosh was designed by Carolyn Davidson in 1971 and cost Nike $35.

In brands we trust

Creating a brand can pay big dividends. A brand generates trust, and ensures that customers keep coming back. Consumers are as loyal to Coca-Cola, Procter & Gamble and Wal-Mart as business users are to Cisco, HSBC and Goldman Sachs.

According to BrandZ consideration of brand in the purchase decision has risen by 20 per cent since 2005, so in uncertain economic conditions people turn to something they can trust – an established brand.

Collect logos that you think appeal to your target audience, and share them with your designer as inspiration for your own design.

Branding is bigger than just a logo design, of course. One brand may have many different designs for different products. The brand is strong enough to tie different projects together. For example:

- ✔ Coca-Cola has the traditional bottle, the tin can, Cherry Cola, Coke Zero and so on. The use of a typeface, the colour red and the iconic ribbon all ensure you recognise a Coca-Cola product.

- ✔ Heinz makes baked beans, soup, ketchup, pickles and many other products. The shape of the label is consistent across all the packaging.

Strapline

A strapline is a short, sharp piece of copywriting that tells people exactly why your business is special. Straplines are incredibly powerful and a good one can become bigger than the business itself and be remembered for a long time! Think about these memorable lines from some of the world's biggest brands:

- ✔ Just Do It.
- ✔ Refreshes the parts other beers cannot reach.
- ✔ Reassuringly expensive.

✔ Your potential, our passion.

✔ Every little helps.

Creating your strapline is closely related to the previous section, about creating a name for your pop up. Use the same list of words. Decide on the main point you want to put across; the most important thing for your customers. Use no more than 6 to 8 words.

Test your ideas on friends, colleagues and existing customers.

Style

Creating a house style is an important part of building a brand that people can recognise. A graphic designer can help you define your style. If you're not using a graphic designer, create a simple guide for yourself. Ensure your house style defines:

✔ How people use your logo. Generally, don't allow your logo to be altered or cropped, and ensure it has some clear space around it in any materials produced.

✔ Any other elements, such as graphic devices, and how they can be used. Decide on the fonts you'll use, and stick to them in all your marketing, including posters and leaflets, signs in the pop up and any materials you produce such as bags.

As a general rule, have one font for your logo, one for headlines and bold text, and one for the general copy in your leaflets. Using standard fonts makes it easy to reproduce this style across everything you do (but make sure the font you use is free and not protected by copyright).

✔ What colours you use. You can choose specific *pantones*, a standard print colour; or for use online, colours are defined as *RGB* – how much red, green and blue is in a colour. From an RGB colour, you can create a six-digit *hex code* to use in websites. You could use a strong colour in your logo across all your marketing, and reproduce it in the look of the shop.

Mastering Marketing

The World Wide Web is full of complex, overly clever definitions of what marketing is and isn't.

The truth is, *marketing* is the way you take your product or service (in this case, your pop up) and sell it to potential customers. Marketing applies your branding to the real world and tells the story of your business. It even finds the people to listen to your story.

Marketing isn't a one-way process; it's not just about talking at people. Your marketing team (which may, of course, be just you) are your eyes and ears as well. Marketing gives you feedback to change, adapt and develop new products. In a pop up, that has to be fast and furious, but if you adapt the agile methods set out in Chapter 2, adapting quickly won't be a problem.

Conducting market research

You've got a great idea for a pop up. You've roughed out your potential audience, so market research is the next step; it helps you check that your idea meets the customers' needs, get some idea of the likely demand, and see whether your pop up is viable. Market research also lets you see some ways you can tweak your plan or your branding to reach a wider audience.

The main aims of market research are to let you see:

- ✔ How big your market is (that is, how many sales you might make).
- ✔ Who your competitors are and how much of the market they have.
- ✔ What kind of customers you may reach and what they might spend.

A whole industry has been built around market research, and big companies spend millions to find out exactly who buys their products and, more importantly, how they can expand their business into new and emerging markets. At the most extreme, expanding your business can involve either developing new products or completely repackaging products.

Assuming that you're not going to employ an expensive market research company, you need to know how to make some decisions about your current and your future audience. You need to draw up an idea of who your audience is, what they like and what influences them. Then you can tailor your marketing to them. (To find out how to determine your audience, see the 'Pinpointing Your Audience' section earlier in this chapter.)

Because pop ups are so short term, you may not have the time for in-depth studies and research, so you need to make informed guesses about your customers. The more informed you become about your customers' likes, wants and aspirations, the more you're able to pitch your pop up in a way that appeals to them.

To find out about your customers:

- ✔ **Spend time where you think your customers gather.** Visit events that they may attend or hang around the cafes you think they like. You can even hang out in the right supermarket aisles!

- ✔ **Don't just hang out in physical locations.** Join Facebook groups and other forums where they might be, even if that means 'Liking' your competitor's page.

- ✔ **Wherever you find them, talk to them, get involved and ask questions.** Just chatting to people often gives you great insight, but make sure you make useful notes so that you can refer back to them in future.

Follow any leads your customers give you; if they talk about a brand you haven't heard of, look it up. If they mention a favourite cafe, visit it.

Over a fairly short timespan, you can gather a snapshot of your customers. Now make sure that your pop up is the kind of thing they'd like!

Finding the right marketing mix

Marketeers is a much better term than marketing professional. A marketeer sounds rather exciting and slightly swashbuckling. And a good marketeer can mix it up a little, juggle lots of balls and keep all the plates spinning at once.

Of course, if you're really lucky, you may have a whole team of skilled marketeers working in-house or an entire company employed to do it for you.

Assuming that you don't have those resources, though, you need to learn to create the right mix of different ingredients to ensure that your message reaches the broadest range of customers or users. You need to do that at the right time and within the right budget, too. You also need to be reaching out to the people who might become customers or users in the future.

To reach the widest audience of customers and potential customers, your marketing mix should include:

- ✔ Press and broadcast media and blogs (see Chapter 9).
- ✔ Social media (see Chapter 8).
- ✔ Print and promotional items (see Chapter 7).

Your market research reveals where you can find your customers, and your marketing mix needs to reflect that research. It should help you reach them, by putting the right items in front of them. If your potential customers are hanging out only on certain websites, that's where to concentrate your mix. If they never go online and spend all their time in cafes, leaflet those places heavily. Of course, the situation is never really that clear cut!

Marketeers need to know how to use lots of different tools. For your pop up, you need proficiency in a range of different skills, or you need to employ people who can do the job better than you. Spending time trying to learn to do something can be more expensive than simply employing somebody else to do it.

What does successful marketing look like?

Be very clear from the start about what successful marketing will look like. You need your marketing to contribute something that furthers your pop up's aim.

You could measure marketing success by the:

- ✔ Number of tweets generated.

- ✔ Amount of 'Likes' a Facebook page gets.

- ✔ Quantity of leaflets distributed in an area.

- ✔ Number of stories in the local press.

- ✔ Total blog posts written.

Of course, these are only numbers; the true measure is whether your pop up gets the number of visitors you aimed for, and whether those visitors help it achieve its overall aim.

Be honest when you come to evaluate your marketing, but don't forget that pop ups are about testing, innovating and prototyping. Testing new things with your pop up marketing is lots of fun, too.

Marketing is a lot of work, so do consider whether other people in your team can contribute to the mix you create by using their own skills and reaching their own networks. (You can find out lots more about building teams in Chapter 3.)

However you tackle it, the trick is in using all the tools, techniques and members of your team to create a balanced, coherent and clear message.

Creating a marketing plan

To manage your marketing, you need to create a plan and ensure that your work has some purpose. Make sure that you're always *on message* – that is, working to fulfil your pop up's aim.

Start a marketing plan with a timetable so that you know what needs to be done, when and by whom. Chapter 2 walks you through setting up a timetable with milestones. A good marketing plan:

✔ Breaks down all the actions required into simple steps and allocates them to a person.

✔ Allows everyone to measure them and makes sure that the project works to an agreed timetable.

✔ Shows any delays or slippages very quickly and lets you adjust your timetable to compensate.

✔ Highlights any points where the workload is heavy and ensures that you can manage those times.

Chapter 7

Producing and Distributing Leaflets and Posters

*R*emember the talk about a paperless office? Well, even in this digital age, getting things printed is still worthwhile.

Giving people a piece of paper is a useful way to open a conversation with strangers, and a VIP invite in the post is still the best way to tell your most valued customers that they're getting special treatment.

Social media is perfect for marketing your pop up and is an invaluable, cost-saving tool. But physical leaflets act as a reminder and a powerful prompt. They get stuck to fridges and nag people to come!

In this chapter, I tell you what you need to know to produce, print and distribute top-notch marketing materials.

Realising Why You Need Printed Materials

Printed materials reach a different audience. They're also a good way to start conversations with staff in businesses that might become keen supporters or even partners in future projects.

As well as marketing, you need to use print in your pop up. Open signs, hanging price labels, menus, point-of-sale displays and carrier bags are all printed items.

Integrate printed materials with your wider campaign; they should all have links to your social media channels and include any tags or hashtags you're using, too (head to Chapter 8 if you're not sure what these are!).

If you get your marketing mix right, people won't be able to move without tripping over your pop up, and good print is a vital part of that process.

Mastering Design Basics

When it comes to design, you need to understand the way things, such as logos, colours and typefaces, look. You need to understand why their appearance matters, too.

You also need to know how those things are applied to a range of different media, from packaging and plastic bags to shop displays and promotional giveaways.

However good your designer is, it's up to you to understand design. And to do that, you need to be inquisitive. Look at things in the world around you – they've all been designed with a purpose in mind.

When you next go shopping, ask some questions:

- ✔ Which things look expensive, and which look cheap? Does this appearance match the actual price difference?

- ✔ What has gravitas and authority, and what looks lightweight and inconsequential?

- ✔ Which products look natural, organic or ecofriendly? Are they really?

✔ What has history and heritage, and what is modern and contemporary?

✔ Which things are everyday and essential, and which are luxury purchases?

How you use design on printed materials can convey all these messages.

Pick things up, hold them and feel them. Why does one thing feel more expensive than another? Why, for example, is a glass bottle of Coca-Cola more valuable than a plastic one? Why is a loaf of bread from the local baker, wrapped in paper, worth more than one from the supermarket that's sealed in plastic?

If you start to look and learn, you can work with your designer to make intelligent, informed choices about your branding and how that's applied to print. You'll understand why decisions about things such as which paper to use for leaflets are important. And you'll produce the best print to support your brand as well.

As you go about your day-to-day life, start collecting examples of design that catch your eye. Pick up flyers, peel labels off jars, take snaps of good posters or shop signs on your mobile phone. Keep an eye out for old ephemera in secondhand bookshops and at car boot sales. Keep all these items in one place – either in a shoe box or set up an account with the Pinterest website (www.pinterest.com), which enables you to display images, videos and more on its pinboard. Not only do you become more literate in design, you'll also be able to brief designers by showing them examples of what you're after. So you'll get better design, too!

Spotting Design Trends

Forecasting design trends is a full-time business, and you don't need to know all the science behind it just for a pop up. However, you want your design work to look fresh, new and contemporary, and that means spotting design trends.

See how design is used in fashion, style and interior design supplements in newspapers and magazines, as well as on popular websites.

You don't need to become an expert, but look for any recurring themes. For example, the ubiquitous 'Keep Calm and Carry On' poster started to appear in a few style supplements before it became a mainstream trend, and 1950s furniture, fabrics and typography were being used by a few magazines in 2011 before becoming mainstream a year later.

Watch out for smaller trends, too. I've recently noticed a number of companies using logos that evoke flags and banners, and a trend for slim, 1930s, industrial typefaces.

Keep your finger on the pulse, and your design will look like it's bang on trend!

Getting the Design You Want

The design process involves various stages. Follow these steps to make sure you end up with the right result:

1. **Conduct research to inform the brief.**

2. **If you're using a designer, give her your brief.**

    You can do this either at a meeting or, better yet, in writing. Your brief outlines what you expect her to do and the total budget. (For more on creating your brief, see the 'Working with a designer' section later in this chapter.)

3. **Research.**

    Your designer will do some research and may come back to you with suggestions to revise the brief. If you're not using a designer, show your brief to family or friends to get their feedback.

4. **Present concepts.**

    Your designer shows you rough, unfinished artwork for you to comment on and choose between designs. Take time and consider what she presents.

5. Finalise the artwork.

Carefully proofread your final design and correct any errors.

6. Print.

You or your designer can deliver artwork to the printer you've chosen. (For more on the printing process, see the 'Printing Your Materials' section later in this chapter.)

Taking It up a Notch: Working with a Good Designer

A good graphic designer brings style, elegance and perhaps even wit to your pop up. She makes sure that you can communicate your message, getting the aim of your pop up across to people. Over time, your designer gets to know what you like and don't like and is able to design work based on that knowledge. A good designer develops a keen sense of what your brand is all about and consistently produces work that you, and more importantly your customers, like.

A good designer can advise you on the many types of print you can produce and help you get the best value for your money as well.

Most of all, a good designer makes sure that your pop up looks professional and stands out from the other shops and all the other information online, too.

Knowing what to look for in a designer

Choosing a graphic designer is very personal; it really comes down to whether you like her and her work at the end of the day. But here are four things to look for when choosing a graphic designer:

✔ **You can see the designer's work.** Ideally, the designer has experience, with a portfolio of work for clients. It's best if these clients have brands similar to the one you want to develop. If the designer is new, she'll have a good collection of work to show you. In either situation, make sure that you like her ideas.

✔ **You can see some common threads in the designer's style of work.** The designer isn't just producing copies of other people's work, but has developed her own style. This style isn't full of generic icons, but is instead distinctive and original.

✔ **The designer communicates well.** She asks you questions about what you're after and listens and responds to your answers. She understands your brief and is willing to question it, if necessary.

✔ **The designer is business-like.** A good designer tells you what you can expect and when. She asks you questions about the timetable and the budget and confirms details in writing.

A good designer walks you through the process of creating your brand, from start to finish. She can help you understand first how to convey your message in an interesting, visual way. Then she'll help you understand things like logos and typefaces, and how they convey different messages.

Finding a designer

The best way to find a designer is to look at work you like and keep an eye open for credits. Many websites include a link to the site's designers, and printed designs often include a discreet design credit.

You can also find plenty of graphic designers online. Spend time browsing sites like Pinterest (www.pinterest.com), where people post things they find eye-catching, to find designers.

You can work with a designer anywhere in the world, and using Twitter, you can ask for suggestions and recommendations. However, you may find working with a local designer easier. Chapter 3 looks at business networking, which is a great place to find local graphic designers or recommendations for them.

Working with a Designer

Saying that design is the most universal of languages, and it surrounds you every day is not to imply that design is easy and everybody should do it. Computers give you tools to design things, but that doesn't mean you're a designer; look at the number of badly laid out posters with fancy fonts on the average noticeboard, and you'll soon recognise the importance of good design.

Good designers can advise you on the many types of print you can use and help you get the best value for your money. Most of all, good designers make sure that your pop up looks professional and stands out from the deluge of information all around it.

You need to give your designer a brief. In it, detail the following:

- ✔ What you want designed.
- ✔ The types of print it will be used for, which determines, for example, suitable typefaces.
- ✔ Quantities of print, as the size of the print run determines the types of technology used.
- ✔ Who your audience is (see Chapter 6).

If your brief is unclear or wrong, your designer won't produce what you need.

You do need to trust designers and remember when briefing them that they should actually design, not just be technicians drawing up something you've penciled out for them. Let designers actually design, and as long as your brief is good, they'll produce work you're happy with.

While you do want to give your designer a brief, show her samples of items you like and identify your audience, you don't want to pre-empt the creative process. Give your designer references but don't be too prescriptive. Give her space to flex her creative muscles!

Talking the talk

Designers, like any specialists, want to tell you that design is a special language, a secret code for the initiated. They'll mumble about the beauty of the ancient goddess Helvetica, and the arcane knowledge of paper weight, pagination and the print process. They may even invoke the Rites of Lithographic, if you let them. The following list, though, helps decipher all this mumbo-jumbo:

✔ *Helvetica* is a clean, simple typeface that designers love.

✔ *Paper weight* is the thickness of the stock; photocopy paper is usually 80gsm, or grams per square metre.

✔ *Pagination* is the process of putting the pages in the right order when printing things with multiple sheets of paper, like books.

✔ *Print process* is the manufacture of your leaflets or posters, and lithographic is one type.

You can find a designer through Freelancers.net (www.free lancers.net/) or People Per Hour (www.peopleperhour. com/find/design). To find a designer on your doorstep, contact your local Chamber of Commerce.

Opting for DIY Design

Of course, you can choose to design your printed materials yourself. You can even produce a lot of your materials in-house; quite literally, as I've been known to turn the kitchen into a temporary printing workshop before a pop up opens!

With simple software, you can produce the artwork you need and cut out the designer altogether. Still follow the process set out in the 'Getting the Design You Want' section earlier in this chapter. It's also worth finding friends or colleagues to give you feedback on your work.

You can go even further with DIY design, though, and be creative. Using stencils, spray paint, stickers and rubber stamps, you can create much of the print you need, from signs and A-boards (see Chapter 10 for more on these) to point-of-sales material and paper bags.

Your DIY designs needn't look any less impressive than the work of a professional designer. Try to create a stylish look and feel that runs right through all the work that you do.

DIY design makes you self-sufficient, too, and if your pop up is personal, quirky or just driven by a particular vision, then it may be the perfect approach for you.

Of course, DIY design is also a great way to save some money. It won't be free; you need to invest in materials to make it look really good. And, of course, it takes some time, too.

 If you choose to take a DIY approach to design, keeping within the branding you've created is really important. (See Chapter 6 for more on branding.) With complete flexibility, bending your brand in all sorts of different ways is very tempting. You can easily end up with a mess of mismatched items, which doesn't help visitors to your pop up. Keep your marketing materials clear, consistent and coherent.

Treat yourself as a designer; write yourself a design brief and make sure that you stick to it!

Designers and DIY design

Even if you've employed a graphic designer, it's unlikely that she'll be able to design every last piece of your pop up. You'll probably want to be able to produce additional items yourself.

If you're clear with your designer that you'll be taking this approach, she can provide the artwork you need in the right format. Being clear from the start also avoids any potential upset later on. Designers can sometimes behave like artists and not like 'their' work being interfered with, altered or adapted.

You can use digital artwork prepared by your designer to create:

- Rubber stamps
- Stencils
- Stickers

You can then use these items to customise your shop and add your branding to a range of objects, from furniture to paper bags.

Consider paying a commercial printing company to complete some of the work, for example printing posters and flyers, as doing so is the most cost-effective way to get the quantities you need to do the job well.

Commissioning a graphic designer while taking a DIY design approach may be what you need. A designer could produce your branding (see Chapter 6) and give you a logo and type-faces to use, and then you could take over designing the actual printed materials using those elements. (For more on this approach, see the sidebar 'Designers and DIY design'.)

Printing Your Materials

After your brand is ready (see Chapter 6) and your designs are created, you can move on to printing.

Don't go to print until you're sure that you like the designs and be careful to proofread everything carefully. Asking some-body who's not directly involved to proofread your leaflets is always worthwhile; you'll be surprised what you can miss because you're so close to the project.

If you're working with a designer, remember that she can help you understand how to get the most beautiful items printed and produced within your budget. A good designer can save you money by advising on the most cost-effective ways to get things printed. And she'll make you money by bringing you more (and maybe even better) customers.

Considering printing techniques

The type of print you use depends on the *print run* – that is, the number of items you need to have printed. Table 7-1 shows you the best options for your needs in a nutshell.

Many printing techniques exist, but the ones you're most likely to need for your pop up are:

- ✔ **Desktop publishing.** This technique is ideal for very short runs. As long as you have a reasonable quality printer, you can produce artwork up to A3 size from your own computer. Remember, printer ink is very expensive, so using your own printer isn't a good idea for print runs that are longer than a few pages! Of course, using your own printer you can customise every single page if you want to. If you need to print more than 25 sheets, use a commercial printer or a copy shop.

- ✔ **Copy shops.** These can produce short runs of leaflets and posters and can provide extra services such as laminating, trimming or binding. They're not cost-effective for larger runs, though. Copy shops are good for things like newsletters and black-and-white flyers. They can also enlarge black-and-white A4 artwork to much larger poster sizes at low cost, which can create some striking visuals in your pop up. Copy shops can also produce full-colour designs in very short runs, such as VIP invites or posters and are most cost-effective for runs of 25 to 100.

- ✔ **Offset lithography, or litho for short.** This is a high-quality technique, and you can carefully match the colours to your artwork. Litho is only cost-effective on larger print runs because the printer makes a plate from your artwork, which is expensive. Litho is the domain of professional printers.

- ✔ **Digital print.** This technique is more cost-effective for shorter runs, but the standard isn't as high as with litho. Digital print can also be turned around quickly and easily. You can personalise digital print – for example, adding customers' names and addresses.

- ✔ **Letterpress printing and screen printing**. These once mainstream commercial printing techniques have now fallen out of use commercially but are still practised as an art. They produce distinct, stylish results but have a higher cost. Letterpress has limited options for design, as you have to use existing typefaces. Screen printing isn't suitable for smaller type.

Table 7-1	Choosing the Printer for Your Needs		
	Desktop	*Copy Shop*	*Commercial Printer*
A4 signs, ten individual designs	X		
10 A5 VIP invites	X		
50 A3 posters		X	
500 black-and-white flyers		X	
100 full-colour folded leaflets			X
5,000 A6 full-colour flyers			X

Budgeting for print

The cost of print varies depending on:

- ✔ Print run
- ✔ Print process
- ✔ Paper type
- ✔ Special requirements

Work out exactly what you need printed and then consider which is the best and most cost-effective way to do so. For runs of about 1,000 full-colour flyers, take the time to shop online. Print brokers, such as www.flyerboy.com, offer highly competitive rates as they place multiple orders with printers to get the best price.

Expect to spend at least 10 per cent of your pop up's total budget on design and print.

Distributing Your Materials

You may have the most beautiful leaflets in the world, but until they're out there and in people's hands, they're not worth anything. It sounds obvious, but good distribution is the key to the success of your print marketing. And it's often forgotten.

You need to get your walking shoes on and take your leaflets around the neighbourhood where your pop up's happening (or pay someone to do it for you!). Hitting the pavement gives you a great opportunity to meet local people and introduce your project. Personally distributing your materials can contribute to the success of your project, not just by helping to create a buzz around your pop up but also by highlighting any local problems you may need to be aware of.

Not every shop and cafe is keen to take leaflets, as some see it as helping a business that's in competition with theirs.

However, if your project has a good community angle, a wider social purpose or is something obviously interesting, people are generally helpful.

Target places that have high footfall and where people can linger and have time to read your print. Good places include:

- ✔ Cafes
- ✔ Pubs
- ✔ Hairdressers and barbers
- ✔ Libraries
- ✔ Bookshops

You can employ distribution companies to circulate your leaflets. However, while it's an effective way of covering a large town or city centre, it's no substitute for getting out there yourself. At the very least, you and your team need to cover the shops neighbouring your pop up.

My first distribution run was for a local theatre, and I distributed leaflets to hundreds of shops for every new season. With 30 shows in each season, I could tailor the right leaflets to the right shops. But my main targets were hairdressers, barbers and local taxi companies; places where people would chat to their customers. I always offered these businesses tickets for the first night, too!

Chapter 8

Making the Most of Social Media

*I*f you're a pop up, you need to mobilise supporters and customers, keep them talking and grow your reputation quickly while you're open. Social media channels are perfect for that, and it's no coincidence that the boom in pop ups has happened at the same time as a rapid growth in the number of people using social media services.

In this chapter, I look at some key social media sites, identify some techniques that make using them easier and more high impact and see why social media is a perfect match for a pop up.

Changing the World with Social Media

Social media – is it just hype or is it really changing the world? Media coverage of social media has been remarkable and veers wildly between being for or against it. So what's the truth – is social media a passing fad, or is it really useful for your pop up?

Here are some facts:

- One out of every eight couples getting married in the United States met on the Internet.
- If Facebook were a country, it would the third largest in the world, behind China and India but ahead of the United States.
- Coca-Cola has 42 million 'Likes' on Facebook.
- Lady Gaga has 24 million followers on Twitter.
- YouTube is the second-largest search engine in the world.
- Every day, 175 million tweets are posted, a quarter of Twitter users check in multiple times, and 11 new accounts are created every second – a million a day.

The Internet accounts for a fifth of all advertising spend in the United States, the world's biggest social media economy. In 2011, while the amount spent on advertising was shrinking by 1 per cent overall, online advertising expenditure grew by 21.2 per cent for the year – even faster than the 12.6 per cent growth posted in 2010.

As people increasingly turn to social media for news, product reviews and to choose restaurants, shows and places to visit, it's obvious that your business needs to have a presence.

So what exactly is *social media*? This term covers all websites and mobile phone apps that enable communication rather than just publishing. Social media includes all sorts of different services, from YouTube to Twitter, but they have certain elements in common.

All social media websites are made up of a blend of seven key elements:

- **Identity:** You can create, maintain and update a personal or business profile.
- **Conversations:** You can communicate with other users.
- **Sharing:** You and other users can exchange, distribute and receive content.
- **Presence:** You can be available online.

Social media versus social networking

A few years ago, a big debate occurred about the difference between social media and social networking. While they were once distinct, with the first about publishing content and the second about building relationships, the two have now converged. People now create and publish content directly onto sites that were once just about creating networks.

- **Relationships:** You can build an affinity with other users, which involves conversing, sharing, meeting up or just appreciating each other.

- **Reputation:** You can create and maintain social media standing, which is recognised by others.

- **Groups:** You can create and join communities or networks with other users.

 Using social media is easy, and it doesn't cost anything to get started – or even to have a big influence. However, it does take time and effort because results are rarely instant. Sign up and set up accounts now, to start getting an understanding of how they work and to build your friends or followers.

 If you're working for a business or organisation, check for any internal guidelines or policies about using social media before you get started.

Understanding Social Media

Social media lets you do two things:

- Build your business brand (see Chapter 6).
- Connect directly with your customers (see Chapter 12).

Using social media, you can convey a huge amount about your business, including not only what you do but also why you do it. You can also explain why you're running a pop up. You can give extra, behind-the-scenes insights that get your customers even more involved, and you can build excitement and buzz before you've even opened the door.

Measuring the impact of social media

Social media is still relatively new, so people are learning more all the time and finding out how to measure what works and what doesn't. A lot of multinationals try to get the highest number of fans or followers, but many people are finding that big numbers aren't a success by themselves. You need those numbers to do something that furthers your pop up's aim.

You can measure success on social media by:

- ✔ The number of fans or followers.

- ✔ The way those fans and followers get involved with your brand.

- ✔ The number of visitors to your pop up.

- ✔ The quantity of comments, posts and pictures generated.

A number of websites are dedicated to helping you measure your impact when using social media. All these sites approach the task of measuring influence and impact in different ways, and learning to use and understand them takes time.

For a beginner, these tools are some of the most useful:

- ✔ **Tweetreach** (www.tweet reach.com) is a simple tool for seeing just how far a tweet or set of tweets has gone, giving you a snapshot of how many people have seen it.

- ✔ **Klout** (www.klout.com) measures your influence based on your ability to drive action on social media. It aims to identify key influencers, people who can affect others by using social media.

- ✔ **Kred** (www.kred.com) goes a little further than Klout by allowing you to factor in achievements in the real world, such as membership of professional organisations.

- ✔ Twenty Feet (www.twenty feet.com) also tracks and measures your social media use, providing easy-to-understand facts and figures.

While all these tools are useful, don't get too hung up on changing the way you use social media to affect your scores; the real measure of success, of course, is whether people come to your pop up!

You can then keep in touch with your customers in real time while the pop up's open and respond to compliments and criticism. You can support and encourage customers to create extra content about your brand, such as videos and photographs, status updates and blog posts. You can help them spread the content you create and the content they create for their networks, too.

And you can ensure that people who can't make it to your pop up still have something to see. You can give people in the next town, next street and even the next country opportunities to see inside your pop up, get involved in what's happening and comment on and create content, too.

Of course, everything you create can stay online – creating a second, wider audience for your pop up and leaving a legacy that people will keep engaging with for years.

Mixing It Up with Social Media

All marketing is about creating the right mix of different ingredients to make sure that your message reaches the broadest range of customers or users. Marketing is also about reaching out to the people who may become customers or users in the future.

Social media sites offers a wide range of different tools, and they can create a variety of types of content. The trick is to use them to create a balanced, coherent and clear message. You need to experiment at first, but then concentrate on the sites that best match your business and its aims.

In this chapter, I give an overview of some useful social media websites. But beware, new sites are appearing all the time, and old ones change the way they work. The only way to become good is just to get stuck in!

Each of the key social media sites has its own etiquette, sometimes enforced by rules but more often informal and agreed by consensus. And they also have their own tone, from the very informal Facebook to the more business-like LinkedIn. Getting the tone right for those different channels takes some time. So by using some or all social media, you can create a mix that reaches the widest possible audience.

Businesses can easily make social media blunders, and they usually happen when the business hasn't invested time in understanding the tone of the users. If you get the tone wrong – for example, by just broadcasting a PR message on a social media site like Twitter rather than interacting with users – then at the very best you'll be ignored. At worst, you'll offend and alienate your customers. Spend some time being quiet and learning the etiquette, tone and popular conventions of social media sites. (To find out more about how to sort out mistakes, see the 'Dealing with problems' section later in this chapter.)

With all social media sites, start by creating a profile. Including a photograph of yourself, not your company logo, is best as social media is about creating personal connections. You need to pay attention to the tone of your social media communications, striking a balance between personal and professional at all times. You can set up separate accounts or profiles purely for your business and keep these more formal for corporate communications. Using the same photo across all sites is a good way to tie them together so think carefully about the picture you choose.

Tweeting on Twitter

Some stories in the press suggest that Twitter's a passing fad, full of people talking about their breakfast. But a number of people have used Twitter to make a real difference, such as the #riotcleanup campaigns following the 2011 riots in the UK. Twitter is powerful because it's really very simple. You can sign up and then create a short profile and a page for all your tweets (short messages). Twitter allows you to post short messages of 140 characters, which other people can read. Other people can follow you to read all your updates, and you can follow them to read their tweets, too. It's not an exchange – you don't have to follow the people who follow you.

For a small website, Twitter has generated an amazing number of newspaper headlines. This suggests that Twitter isn't just a useful tool for reaching customers, but you can also use it to get your story to the media.

Generally, the tone on Twitter is positive. Lots of people share links to content, and sharing good content is the quickest way to get people to follow you. On Twitter, lots of people respond to questions and use the platform to collaborate.

Twitter is frequently criticised as all trivia and nonsense. But if you overhear any sentence in a conversation out of context, it would probably sound the same! Eavesdropping on Twitter conversations is perfectly acceptable, so do read the tweets before and after a message and also look at other people's tweets so that you can follow a conversational thread.

Setting up an account

An estimated 10 million Twitter accounts are active in the UK. Some accounts are simply people just chatting to friends, while others are big brands promoting their products.

Anyone can set up an account, and it's free. If a message is interesting enough, other Twitter users follow that account for future messages. If other people like what they read, they *retweet* (usually abbreviated to RT) and pass the message to their followers. You can follow almost all accounts; very few people keep their accounts private.

Using hashtags

You can easily filter messages if users add *hashtags* – a word or phrase preceded by the # symbol. Keep your hashtag short and simple, so it doesn't use up too much of your 140-character limit. Hashtags make it easy to search Twitter and follow a conversational thread. You can also embed a stream of tweets with a set hashtag in your own website using Twitter's basic widgets.

No official central register of hashtags exists, so check by doing a search before creating one for your pop up. If you want to create a unique stream of tweets that are just about your pop up, you need to find something that nobody is using. If you want to join in a wider conversation, you can use existing hashtags, and your tweets are read by people following that stream.

For pop up shops, use existing hashtags like:

- #emptyshops
- #popupshop
- #popuppeople

People can also read tweets without using the Twitter website. For example, many websites have a stream of live tweets embedded in them, and many events, such as conferences, project tweets on the wall for people to read.

Twitter provides easy-to-use tools and widgets to allow you to embed your tweets or feeds in your own website. You can display rolling feeds, which update automatically, either of your own tweets or searches of general terms or hashtags. The more you can share Twitter feeds and streams, the more useful Twitter is!

For more on Twitter, go to: `https://twitter.com/about/resources`

Socialising on Facebook

Facebook appears to be a complicated site to use, with lots of different functions. To make it even more tricky, the site changes regularly as new features and functions are added. However, Facebook is the biggest of the social networks, with an estimated 900 million users around the world, so navigating it can't be that hard!

You don't need to become a Facebook black belt, you just have to find out how to use the bits that deliver results for you.

Getting started

The first step in using Facebook is to register. You then create a personal profile.

Make this profile as complete as you're comfortable with, but don't give away personal information if you don't want to.

After you have a Facebook account, you can add other users as friends, exchange messages, and post status updates – including text, video, pictures or links. All this functionality means that, for some people, Facebook has become synonymous with the Internet; they do everything within it.

Just like on Twitter (see preceding section), lots of people share links to good content, and sharing good content is the quickest way to get to know like-minded people.

Using Facebook Pages and Groups

As well as your personal profile, Facebook lets you create or subscribe to a separate Page. Pages are commonly used to promote a business, a project or an online shop. Pages are visible to everyone, even those who haven't signed up to use Facebook. Facebook users can click a Like button to follow a Page's updates.

Facebook Pages are very similar to normal profiles on the site – a Page can have friends, add pictures and have a Wall for fans to post on. Pages are separate from the person who created them.

Facebook also allows people to create or subscribe to a Group. Groups are more closely identified with the person who started them and are more like a private club; you can choose who can and cannot join a Group. Groups can therefore be a private space for discussion and sharing links or other information about a particular topic, project or cause.

Groups are great for organising on a more personal level, so it may be worth setting one up so that everyone involved in your pop up can communicate. Pages are better for brands, businesses and the like who want to interact with fans or customers without having them connected to a personal account. Creating a Page for your pop up is definitely worth it.

Creating a Like box

One major difference between Facebook and Twitter is that what happens in Facebook tends to stay in Facebook, while Twitter content can be taken and embedded in other websites much more easily. Be careful about creating all your content in Facebook as it's hard to remove it later, and it can't be shared outside Facebook's users easily.

The one way content can be taken outside of Facebook is by creating a Like box. You can easily embed this feature into your website, so that all of your online communications join up. Like the widgets Twitter offers, this box can be created simply on the Facebook website without lots of technical skill and then embedded in your website.

For more information, go to: `http://developers.face book.com/docs/reference/plugins/like-box/`

Uploading Pictures to Flickr

By August 2011, Flickr hosted 6 billion images, with more being added all the time. Unlike the complexity of Facebook, Flickr does one thing: enable people to upload their photos, sort them into sets and allow other people to view them. You can also upload video, but this function isn't used as much as most people prefer to use social media sites dedicated to film, such as YouTube and Vimeo.

You don't need to set up an account to see other people's pictures, but you do need one to upload content onto the website. Uploading is simple, thanks to tools that let you pick photos from your computer. You can tag photographs to help people find them, add titles, write a short description and sort them into sets. You can also pin notes to an individual photograph. All your photos make up your *photostream*.

After you have an account, you can create a profile page showing your photostream. You can also add other Flickr users as contacts and see all your contacts' recent photos in one place.

Flickr users can also create Groups – for example, around a theme, style or place. Other users can join a Group and add their photos to it. You can also add comments on other people's photos and mark pictures as Favourites.

Flickr has two account types:

- ✔ **Free:** As a Free account user, you can add 300MB of images and two videos per month and can see only the most recent 200 in your photostream.

- ✔ **Pro:** With a Pro account, you can upload an unlimited number of images and videos every month.

In addition, you can use Flickr to host images for other blogging sites. You can also create widgets that allow you to display photos from an individual feed, a specific set or from a Group on your own website.

For a pop up, Flickr is useful in two ways:

- ✔ You can add your own photographs and then embed them in your pop up's website.

- ✔ You can create a Group and invite people visiting your pop up to add their photographs.

Working with Video on YouTube

If Flickr is the best place for photos, YouTube is the venue for video (although a number of people are moving to Vimeo, which I discuss in the next section).

You don't need to set up a YouTube account to see other people's videos, but you do need one to upload content onto the website.

Uploading is simple, using tools that let you pick film from your computer. You can tag the videos you upload to help people find them, add titles, write a short description and sort them into playlists.

On YouTube, your profile page is called, appropriately enough, your *channel*. You can follow other people's channels, including certain people's videos and the comments on those videos.

After you set up your channel, you can customise it. YouTube gives you considerable flexibility over colours, page layouts and so on, so that you can create a channel that looks distinct and stylish, adding your pop up's branding as an icon or a background image as well. However, the player (the box that includes your video and the controls) always has YouTube's branding.

Just as on Twitter and Flickr, you can easily embed videos from YouTube into your own website or even into other social media sites. YouTube makes the code for this task available, allowing for everything from simple embeds to more complicated integrations.

YouTube is the second-biggest search engine in the world, used to find and view 3 billion videos every day. While YouTube has the potential to reach a massive audience, it's more likely that your video will be lost in the crowd! If you use You Tube, don't expect an immediate audience and be prepared to use other social media to bring people to view your video.

YouTube is a good way to show off your pop up and reach a wider audience – including people around the world who won't be able to make it to your pop up while it's open. You can use YouTube to offer extra behind-the-scenes insights and interviews with key partners or even just customers, building on your brand. You can also use YouTube to create a legacy, meaning your pop up lives on after it's closed.

Adding Video with Vimeo

Vimeo is like YouTube's little brother. It's a slightly more refined version of the service, with some advantages in terms of the technical quality of videos.

As with YouTube, you need to create an account to add video to Vimeo. You can follow people, which means you subscribe to their videos, receive updates and have the ability to send them messages.

One of the main advantages of Vimeo over YouTube is the way it allows you to create Groups. These communities are built around videos and other things that people like. You can create your own Groups or join other people's.

Another advantage of Vimeo is the degree of customisation it offers, even allowing you to brand the player with your own logo.

Just like YouTube, Vimeo is a good way to show off your pop up and reach a wider audience – including people who won't be able to make it to your pop up while it's open. If you add extra behind-the-scenes insights and interviews, Vimeo's active community can discuss them. And Vimeo, as with YouTube, means your pop up lives on after it's closed.

Growing Up with LinkedIn

The Facebook for grown-ups is how LinkedIn is often seen. It's a useful site for making professional connections and for finding ways to connect with other people in business.

As with other sites, you need to sign up to create a profile. With LinkedIn, you can create only one profile, and it must be personal; you don't create separate pages for personal and business, for example.

Try to complete as much of your profile as possible. Do include a photo. After all, this is a business networking site, and you wouldn't turn up at an event in the real world wearing a balaclava!

After you sign up, you can find and create connections, searching for people you know or people who work in a business sector you're interested in. You should create a personal message each time, rather than using the default message provided.

LinkedIn policy is that you're supposed to know those people you contact. However, it's hard to match that with the goal of building a network of people who share common interests and experiences. Be careful about approaching total strangers as doing so can result in being removed from the LinkedIn site.

Managing Social Media

Using social media delivers massive benefits, but it's not free and easy. You have to invest time, and you need to make a commitment to update the sites you use regularly.

The biggest commitment is to managing the various channels you choose to use. You need to see, track and respond to any comments you receive. You can't use all your time just managing those accounts, so you need to make sure that you have the biggest impact with the smallest investment of time.

And if you're working with partners, you need to make sure that you all communicate, across all the channels available, to build your pop up's brand.

Thankfully, plenty of tools help you manage your social media profile.

Dashboards

Tweetdeck and Hootsuite are two useful tools for making sense of Twitter, Facebook and all the content they generate. They allow you to create a dashboard to control your many accounts. They sort updates across your social media sites into columns, which update automatically – the people you follow, and searches for keywords that are of interest, for example. This means you can easily see and manage a wide range of content.

Particularly useful are geographical searches, which enable you to see people using social media near to your pop up.

Both tools allow you to post to Twitter and Facebook and manage multiple accounts so that you can maintain lots of contact from one place and differentiate between, for example, a personal account and one set up for your pop up.

Tweetdeck is an application you install on your computer or mobile, so it has some limitations if you're moving between different devices. Hootsuite is a web-based application. However, Tweetdeck is owned by Twitter and is testing a web-based version.

Both tools let you post scheduled updates, so you can send content to your social media networks even when you're away from your desk. Obviously, Tweetdeck has a disadvantage, being tied to one machine, as it only sends them if your computer is turned on.

Google Alerts

All day, every day, people are creating new content online, and as soon as it's created, Google starts finding it. Google Alerts at www.google.com/alerts sends you a notification when new content is found.

You can set up searches for anything: your business name, the place where you're opening a pop up or keywords relating to what your pop up does. You can even choose how often you receive alerts, and they're mailed directly to your inbox.

Google Alerts are particularly useful for monitoring what's said about your business and your pop up. But these alerts also find regular fresh, interesting content for specialist subjects, which you can share across your social media channels, making you an instant expert in your field!

Mobile

Most social media websites have mobile versions so that you can Tweet, upload photos to Flickr, update your Facebook status and post films on YouTube from any smartphone. You can even do some of it with an older phone, using text messaging.

Look at the mobile versions of each social media channel you use; they're particularly useful for creating instant content live from your pop up.

Planning Social Media

Social media relies on interaction, so you can't ever predict exactly how it's going to work out. You need to be agile, responding to opportunity and grabbing the chances you're given by the people you interact with.

However, you can create a plan and ensure that your communications via social media have some purpose!

Creating a plan for using social media is closely related to the aims and objectives that I talk about in Chapter 2, and this exercise works with the timetable from that chapter (Table 2-1). Of course, it should also relate to your branding and marketing (see Chapter 6).

Creating a message grid

To create a social media plan, refer to the process described in Chapter 2.

After you do so, you need to match your messages to those milestones. The easiest way is to create a message grid, commonly used by politicians during an election campaign but very useful for anybody who's spreading communications across a period of time.

Lots of everyday interaction occurs as well – people won't be interested if you just say one thing over and over! Match your message to the tone and style of the channel you're using.

After you have a message grid that tells you what messages need to be pushed and when, make sure that you share it with all your partners. If you're all pushing together, you can create a more powerful campaign around your pop up.

Creating messages and campaigns

After you know what you need to say and when, you need to look at how you'll say it. To be really effective, you want other people using social media to pick up your message. When Shakespeare made a character in *Twelfth Night* say '[I'll] Halloo your name to the reverberate hills/ And make the babbling gossip of the air/ Cry out', he obviously wasn't talking about social media; but it *is* a good way to think about it! You want to be loud at times, but you also want lots of babble and conversation, which is quieter.

You want to spread your message across as many channels as possible, tailoring it to the tone and style they use – as well as the medium. A campaign that really takes off in this way goes *viral*, which means that it keeps spreading as lots of users share, repost and pass on the content – and that's the Holy Grail of social media.

The first step in creating a campaign is to write a clear, simple and easy-to-share message for each stage of your message grid.

Remember to:

- ✔ Use plain English.
- ✔ Be clear.
- ✔ Excite people.
- ✔ Keep it short enough for sharing.

Make your messages short enough for a tweet, so aim for 120 to 140 characters in length. This message is the basic version; on Facebook and other sites, you can build on this foundation.

Think about how to use different channels to convey your message:

- ✔ On Facebook, be friendly and informal.
- ✔ On Flickr, use a photo or set of photos that can get your message across, such as an image of empty shops in the area you're planning to pop up. As well as posting these photos on Flickr, share them on Facebook and on your blog.
- ✔ On YouTube or Vimeo, post a short film, perhaps looking at the problem your pop up solves or at the geographical area you'll be working in. You can share this film on YouTube, Vimeo, Facebook and your blog.

 If you're creating a tweet that you want people to share – called a retweet – it needs to be about 120 characters long, not the full 140 characters. This leaves people enough room to add 'RT @yourname' at the start of their tweet.

Dealing with problems

You've probably heard about brands getting into trouble when they get social media wrong or they have a problem and social media amplifies it.

The solution is, of course, simple: don't do things badly in the first place! Social media itself rarely causes the problem. Problems on social media are usually a sign that the company is doing something wrong elsewhere. But because social media is open, it's easy to complain, and content is shared quickly and widely. In the old days, only the company would know how many customers complained by letter or phone call, but now those complaints happen very publicly.

If your pop up is good, well-planned and carried out carefully, you're unlikely to make major mistakes. And if you've built good relationships with your fans and followers, they're unlikely to turn on you if a problem occurs. In fact, you may find that they turn into keen supporters, and calm down a situation without your intervention.

However, if you do run into problems:

- ✔ Be nice.
- ✔ Keep all your communication public.
- ✔ Be honest with people.
- ✔ Apologise if you've made a mistake.

Chapter 9

Cooking Up a Media Storm for Your Pop Up

• •

In This Chapter

▶ Developing a media plan of action

▶ Figuring out what the media wants (and delivering it)

▶ Coming up with a compelling press release

▶ Working with both traditional and new media

• •

*M*ore media outlets exist today than ever before. Everybody can be their own media hub, publishing blogs, shooting and sharing videos, uploading audio and spreading it wide for their own audiences. Canadian philosopher and writer Marshall McLuhan predicted that, 'The age of automation is going to be the age of *do it yourself*', and it seems he was right.

And the old media – TV channels, radio stations, magazines and newspapers – are still around. In fact, many towns have their own local listings magazines. My home town has five, all serving different audiences, as well as two local newspapers.

In this chapter, I look at how to write both a media campaign plan and a press release, and how to find the right people to contact. I also show you how to tailor your content for the traditional media and how to engage with those working in new media – the bloggers, film-makers and others who are taking McLuhan's DIY approach.

Planning a Media Campaign

Before you start on your media plan, be really clear about what you hope to achieve. Overall, your campaign must further the aim of your pop up. But in more detail, it may well be that your media plan helps you achieve individual objectives, too. For example, you can use part of your media campaign to recruit volunteers to help staff your pop up or find local producers whose goods you can stock. While they help you tick off a job that needs doing, those stories also contribute to achieving the bigger aim.

The messages you send to journalists are called *press releases*, no matter what type of medium you're sending them to. A press release, which is sometimes referred to as a *media release*, reads like an article in a newspaper.

If you create a plan for delivering press releases, you can ensure that:

- ✓ Your press releases are always sent on time.
- ✓ They reach the right journalists.
- ✓ You can measure the success of each individual release.
- ✓ The momentum around your pop up builds before you open and continues when you close.

Creating a media plan is closely related to the aims and objectives that I talk about in Chapter 2 and your use of social media, which I talk about in Chapter 8. Of course, it should also relate to your branding and marketing (see Chapter 6). In short, your media plan must work with the other parts of your pop up, and not be treated in isolation.

To create your media plan:

1. **Write the aim of your pop up at the top of the page.**

   All your communication needs to be about helping you achieve this aim.

2. **Draw a timeline down one side of the paper, starting with today's date and ending after your pop up closes.**

3. **Mark the opening date and closing date on your timeline.**

4. **Sketch in the key milestones leading up to the opening.**

   You can find out more about identifying these milestones in Chapter 2.

5. **Make sure that your press releases are ready at the right times, by matching them to those milestones.**

   Some journalists, particularly those working on monthly or quarterly magazines, need your press releases at least two to three months in advance. (See the 'Writing press releases' section later in this chapter for more information.)

Table 9-1 shows a sample media plan.

Table 9-1	A Sample Media Plan	
Timeline	*Milestones*	*Message*
1st March	Create plan	Start contacting media. Target monthly magazines. Send first press release about organisation
13th April	Confirm location	First press release about pop up out to all journalists
16th April	Start marketing	Target selected local journalists for interviews, more detailed editorial pieces
19th May	Open	Invite journalists to opening party
19th May onwards	Interviews and photos	Interviews at pop up with journalists; photo call on location. Shoot photos for future press releases
15th June	Return keys	Conclusions and achievements press release

After you have a timetable, you can see:

- ✓ How many press releases you need to write.
- ✓ The dates these releases need to be written and sent to journalists.
- ✓ How they help you achieve the objectives in your overall plan.

You'll have lots of everyday interaction with journalists as well, particularly using social media channels. If you make contact with a new journalist, send him your last press release to help bring him up to speed with your pop up.

I've separated *new media* from *social media* because new media is much more akin to old journalism. New media is about creating and publishing good content, whether it's the written word, film or audio. Social media is more about sharing and distributing that content. Of course, some overlap exists, and the boundaries of the old media, new media and social media are becoming more blurred all the time.

Getting into the Minds of the Media

Sometimes it seems as if the media are something apart from the rest of society. The media seem to have their own ways of working, a different language and a huge amount of influence. But nobody who works in the media would be anything without people feeding them good stories. As long as you can identify what makes a good story, you won't have any problem getting the media to give your pop up valuable coverage.

Working with the media is a full-time job and the skills you need can be hard to learn. However, people who run pop ups need to be good generalists with a working knowledge of lots of different areas.

Recognising what makes a story

All journalists are after a good story, and your pop up will only get good media coverage if you present it to journalists as such. What makes a good story varies, of course, depending on what the writer (and the publisher) thinks her readers are interested in. So the press release you send to a specialist publication, such as a trade magazine, needs to be very different from the one that you send to your local newspaper.

Journalists are busy people. The number of staff at most newspapers, TV studios and radio stations has been cut in recent years, yet they have even more work to do. For example, newspapers don't just have column inches to fill once a week; they also have to fill blogs with daily content and shoot films, too.

This need for content means that you have a great opportunity. If you can give the media good stories, tailored to their style and their audience, they'll be very happy to give you some space. Learn to do journalists' work for them. If you don't make your pop up relevant to the media's readership, then the journalist may think, 'Just buy an ad!'

Remembering the Five Ws

You need to give journalists the information they need in a way they can understand, and it must always include the Five Ws:

- ✔ **Who** is organising the pop up.
- ✔ **What** is happening.
- ✔ **When** it takes place.
- ✔ **Where** the pop up will be.
- ✔ **Why** it's happening.

If you can answer all five, you've got a complete story. But if you forget one of the Five Ws, you have a hole in your story. Imagine reading about a pop up, but the 'when' was missing – you wouldn't know when to turn up. And if the 'what' was missing, you probably wouldn't be interested in the first place!

Knowing your angle

You need the Five Ws and a good angle to get your story published. A good angle is like the bait on a fishing hook; it's what makes your story appeal to a particular journalist.

Spotting media opportunities

Keep an eye open for good opportunities to promote your story.

Generally, ignore vague opportunities such as 'it's National Rubbish Week' or 'today is International Cheese Day', as journalists are given lots of these stories. Don't try to hitch your pop up to the wrong wagon, either; nothing's worse than seeing a brand trying to cash in on a major news story.

But if a story in the national press relates in some way to your pop up, do write a release or contact journalists you know on social media.

I managed to get great press coverage for artist Adrian Crick because he had a painting in a pop up exhibition at Brighton's West Pier, based on a jumbled collage of photographs. When that historic structure collapsed into the sea, the pop up exhibition featuring his work (which now looked prophetic!) suddenly became far more interesting to the press.

An angle may be that the story is:

- ✔ Local
- ✔ Topical
- ✔ Part of a bigger story
- ✔ Quirky or unusual

Writing press releases

If you want to grab a journalist's attention, you need to write a good, clear press release (see the later example). Your press release must be short and sharp and include all the information you need to tell the story.

Press releases always need to answer the Five Ws (see the 'Remembering the Five Ws' section earlier in this chapter). They need to read like an article in a newspaper, with the most important information right at the top.

Here's how to write a punchy press release in seven simple steps:

1. **At the top of your press release, include the name of your group or project, the date and the words Press Release.**

2. **Add an attention-grabbing headline.**

    A maximum of half a dozen words is ideal. Think like a tabloid. The headline will probably explain the angle of the story.

3. **Write your first paragraph.**

    Keep the first paragraph short (just one line is good), outlining the story in an interesting way. Use bold to make this paragraph stand out from the page and grab interest. If you don't get attention now, your press release will end up in the bin – or turned into a NIB, a News In Brief piece, at the side of the page.

4. **Follow up with some background and then lead in to the story.**

    Explain what's happening and why it's of interest to readers. Aim to write a press release that's between 300 to 400 words. If it's too short, your press release won't get good coverage; if it's too long, it won't get read. Remember the Five Ws.

5. **Restate the most important facts in a quote from someone involved in your project.**

    Make sure it sounds like something that somebody might actually say, though!

6. **Make it clear where the story ends and that any following information is additional and for the press only.**

    Using '/ends' is standard and easy to understand. Add your contact details and any Notes for Editors, such as the background to a pop up, a list of funders or a brief history of a venue.

7. **Offer a good photo to match the story.**

    Provide an actual photo and also offer the press the opportunity to take their own. A good picture really makes your story stand out. Offer interviews or live broadcast ideas for radio and TV.

While museum celebrates 100 years, new gallery pops up

Worthing Museum and Art Gallery has just marked its 100th year, but the organisers of a new gallery in Worthing have slightly more modest ambitions.

Worthing Museum and Art Gallery has just marked its 100th year, but the organisers of a new gallery in Worthing have slightly more modest ambitions.

Revolutionary Arts are planning a Pop Up Gallery, which will be open to the public for just four days. Next Wednesday 1st April, artists will get the keys to a shop in Worthing's Guildbourne Centre and will open an art gallery the next day. And at the end of Sunday 5th April, the gallery will close its doors for the last time.

The gallery will include gritty black-and-white photography, dramatic paintings, installation art and digital illustrations. Much of the work will be for sale, and there will be hand-made cards, badges and locally published poetry books, too.

It's not a unique project – the group has opened galleries in empty shops before, and pop ups are part of a worldwide movement that finds new uses for empty shops.

However, the short time the gallery will be open makes it unusual, and while it would be easy to miss, it should be unmissable for local art aficionados.

'We have a crack team of high-speed curators working right now,' says exhibition organiser Dan Thompson, 'to make sure we bring together the best contemporary artists for a stunning (if short) show!'

The Pop Up Gallery will be in Unit 13, The Guildbourne Centre, Worthing and will be open from 11am–4pm, Thursday 1st–Sunday 5th April.

For more information, visit www.artistsandmakers.com

/ends

Contact Revolutionary Arts for photographs, biographies of the artists involved and interview opportunities.

Revolutionary Arts works with artists and others to create pop up exhibitions and events in unlikely spaces.

If you work in a larger business or organisation, you more than likely have a press officer to write and mail a press release for you. This person has spent time building relationships with journalists and knows what sort of stories they're looking for. Consider this person to be a key partner in your work and keep her informed early and often about your pop up.

If you don't have access to a press officer and really dread the thought of distributing media releases, consider using a professional agency to write and distribute press releases for you. This great investment can return real results. If you have a local agency, you may be able to persuade them to come onboard with your project and work at a lower rate than they would for a commercial client.

Check out www.journalism.co.uk/skills/s7/ for tips on writing press releases, and getting noticed by journalists.

Making Contacts

Building a good list of email contacts in the local and regional media is fairly easy to do. Buy newspapers, pick up free magazines and scour websites for email addresses. Update your lists regularly and add other journalists as you discover or meet them.

After you have a list of contacts, don't overuse them, but do be prepared to spend time building relationships. Don't expect instant results just because you've sent somebody a press release: journalists don't work for you!

Create a list in your email address book (such as Outlook or Thunderbird) to make it easier to mail your press release to multiple accounts. Always include addresses you gather in the 'BCC' (blind carbon copy) field, which means they're kept private.

Networking with journalists using social media

Social media channels like Twitter and Facebook give you direct routes to journalists as well. To build relationships with journalists on social media:

- Follow them, not just by clicking a button but by reading their articles. Understand what they're interested in and what they write about.

- Share other articles by them with your networks.

- Comment on what they say. Be polite and friendly. Don't try to push your point.

- Send them links to things that might interest them, such as blog posts or photographs. Don't just push your own work.

Don't approach journalists on social media completely cold. Warm them up before you ask them to help publicise your pop up.

Distributing media releases

Distributing emails by press release is perfectly acceptable. Include a summary and your contact details in the body of the email, with the full press release attached as a document. The press release can either be a Word document or a pdf. In either case, avoid loading it with too many graphics or images. Press releases are about the words.

Set press releases in 10 to 12 point type, using a standard font like Arial or Times New Roman. Fancy fonts you use may not be installed on other people's computers so may be lost.

Attach one or two good images to your press release, but do check the file size so that you don't make people's email accounts crash!

As well as distributing your press release to any lists you've collated, you can utilise services that distribute press releases. Some are free for a basic service, but most charge a fee per release or a membership fee (see Table 9-2).

Table 9-2	Press Distribution Services
Paid Services	**Free Services**
www.prweb.com	www.free-press-release.com
www.prfire.co.uk	www.i-newswire.com
www.prnewswire.co.uk	www.onlineprnews.com

Following up

Like everything else, success in your communications is nearly always down to making friends and keeping in touch with them.

Keep in touch with journalists using social media. But do try not to hassle them; keep it friendly and polite but don't bury them in press releases or make them feel you're being too pushy.

After emailing a release, drop them a tweet saying that you've emailed them. Offer anything further they might need.

Always follow any coverage you get (whether you're happy with the amount of space you received or not!) with a thank you note, either by email or using social media.

Making the Most of Traditional Media

You could almost think that the traditional media are irrelevant. But while it's a time of change for print media (newspapers and magazines) and broadcast media (radio and television), they're still influential.

What you're after when contacting these people is *editorial coverage*, written by journalists. Editorial coverage is free and distinct from advertising; be wary of any offers of content based on you buying advertising space. Editorial includes reviews, features, interviews and comment pieces.

While new media like blogs and community websites have big followings and people on social media have a huge influence, the traditional media still have authority, credibility and real clout.

And that's not just at a national level. While getting a write-up in a major, national paper would be a great achievement, it's not an easy thing to secure. Local media are just as important; they bring with them a loyal audience. They're also the place where many of the stories you read in the national press were found!

In most places, councillors and council officers are still in awe of print and broadcast journalists, even if local bloggers attract far more readers. If you're looking for help from your local council, the extra work involved in getting the traditional media talking about your pop up is worth it.

Local papers have a substantial readership, around 40 million adults a week, are affordable to advertise in and have a focused readership. Hold The Front Page (www.holdthefrontpage. co.uk/directory/) has links to the 200 or so local daily and weekly papers from the *Aberdeen Evening Express* to the *York Herald*.

Gaining New Media Coverage

You have a pop up to design, a marketing plan to implement, stock to source and a lease to sign. How much time should you give to persuading somebody who writes a blog to write about your pop up?

New media are the noisy young upstarts that are upsetting the old media. Anyone can start a blog, launch a podcast or broadcast news films online.

While many people do that and just talk to a few friends, other blogs have huge followings. This is particularly true where people gather round a particular interest or campaigning theme.

Just as you need to know what the traditional media want in a story, so you also need to know what new media are after. You don't want to waste the little time you have chasing new media opportunities if you're creating content for sites nobody sees.

Look for blogs that have a regular readership. You can judge readership through the number of views individual stories attract, on sites where such statistics are on view. Otherwise, look for:

- ✔ Regularly updated content.
- ✔ A large number of people linking to the site.
- ✔ A good number of positive comments on articles.

In particular, target your content to the needs of blogs writing for a niche market. For example, if you're reusing an old shop in a city centre, look for blogs that are written specifically about that area or that focus on pop up projects.

The people who write blogs for niche markets are often enthusiasts who love their subject and are experts in everything to do with it. If you can match your pop up with their passion, they'll not only write about it but also spread the word, pass the article to their networks and generally act as your pop up's champion.

Part IV
Running Your Pop Up

The 5th Wave   By Rich Tennant

Art's AUTO PARTS

GIFT BASKETS

Gasket Greetings | Valentine Tune-Up | Spark-Plug Sampler

SALE
~~1/3 OFF~~
1/2 OFF

"I don't know, Art. I think you're just ahead of your time."

In this part . . .

For many people, shopping today is a leisure activity; as much entertainment as practical. People use the supermarket for the day-to-day things, and want something extra from the shopping they do in their spare time. And pop ups are part of that trend, providing something interesting and unusual among the usual shops.

So you need to deliver a good experience for your visitors! In this part, I look at how to make your pop up an interesting, well-designed and effective space. I talk through how your pop up team can work together to deliver good customer service. Finally, I help you to make sure that visitors to your pop up become good customers for your business.

Chapter 10

Designing and Kitting Out Your Space

*R*eady to get really creative; to unleash the dogs of interior design and have some fun? Good, because pop up shops are all about being creative, and kitting out your shop, creating displays and designing windows is where that creativity comes to the fore.

In this chapter, I mix very practical stuff, such as tips for decorating, with some more cerebral notions about the psychology of store layouts. Remember, though, that kitting out your shop is all about creating something unique, and not every solution will fit every space.

Creativity Counts

When you're working on the high street, you've got to look good. High-street retailers spend a lot of time, money and effort making their shops as appealing as possible. You can achieve similar standards on a budget by being creative and thinking sideways.

In fact, while it was creative people who started kitting out shops using recycled wooden pallets and old furniture, some very trendy brands have applied the look in their own stores. Look inside a Cath Kidston shop to see recycled furniture and quirky curation of the available space. Jack Wills stores look like they've been lifted lock, stock and leather armchair from a country house. And visit a Superdry shop, which make its shops look like they're furnished with old industrial stuff, even having battered oil drums painted in their corporate colours. Ten years ago, that 'recycled chic' would have been unheard of in mainstream shops.

So if you're really creative, you may just inspire the big shops to copy you. As the writer Quentin Crisp said, 'Never keep up with the Joneses – drag them down to your own level'!

Whatever the rules are, the golden rule is always that there are no rules. While some people love a clean, chic boutique with a few well-placed items, others are much happier shopping in a higgledy-piggledy junk shop, where things are piled floor to ceiling. Some like custom-made furniture to show off high-class products and others want to use a pile of old timber to create a funky space.

You need to find the shop design, style and layout that fits your aim, your brand and your customers.

Designing the Shop Front

The front of your shop is vitally important, as it makes a big statement to anyone passing by. It's the first chance you have to get your brand across. Get the look of your shop front wrong, and you'll soon find it was the last chance you had, too. Get it right, and you'll be inviting people to step through the door of your pop up. Your footfall will increase, and the busier your shop looks, the keener other passers-by will be to come in. You'll notice that a busy shop just keeps getting busier; it's getting the first few people in that's difficult.

It really is true that people won't set foot in an empty shop, but walk into a busy one to see what's going on. Create the most activity at the front of your shop, perhaps by making a social space or locating your sales desk here. You can find out lots more about designing the space and creating zones in the 'Inside the Shop' section later in this chapter.

Get the look wrong, and customers are put off from investigating your shop. They won't know whether you're open or understand what you're doing, and they won't come in. You'll be alone inside, watching a procession of people gazing with a look of bewilderment (or worse, indifference) at your shop.

By the way, even when the shop's closed, a good shop front encourages people to stop and grabs their interest. And you can use new technology, such as a QR (quick response) code (a code you scan with your smartphone to take you to a website), so that a closed shop still engages with customers.

High-street retailer Marks & Spencer teamed up with the charity Oxfam to launch the Shwop project, highlighting the fact that one in four items of clothing bought goes to landfill and encouraging people to drop items into in-store recycling bins. As part of the launch, Marks & Spencer opened Shwop Lab, a pop up shop showcasing sustainable fashion. But it also created window displays in stores across the country to highlight the initiative, and these displays featured a QR code linking to further information. Even when stores were closed, passers-by could engage with the project.

Security shutters

Some shops come with heavy steel security shutters that roll down when you're closed. These shutters do make your shop secure and give you peace-of-mind when you're closed. But they're very ugly and often make a neighbourhood feel unfriendly; they suggest that the area isn't safe.

In the North Laine area of Brighton, many of the shops' shutters have been spray painted by local artists. The streets look more lively and colourful when closed, and the shops stand out even when they're shut. If your shop is fitted with shutters, see whether you can get permission to paint them. Do use a professional artist to do the work, as you'll get a much better end result. Make sure that you mask the shop front thoroughly before painting, as most shutters let paint through!

Graffiti in the White House

Ben Eine is a London street artist who specialises in the central element of all graffiti – the form of letters. He spent a year working with shopkeepers in Middlesex Street, in the Spitalfields area of London. Eine painted a whole alphabet on 26 shop shutters, in bold typography and cheerful colours. The site has become a popular destination for art lovers. Since then, Eine has produced work for commercial clients and contemporary galleries. And Prime Minister David Cameron presented one of his works to US President Obama as a gift on his first official state visit to the UK.

External decoration

Redecorating or redesigning your shop front doesn't need to be expensive. You can do a great job yourself or employ a professional. Whatever you do:

- ✔ Keep it clean.
- ✔ Keep it simple.

The shop available may be in a prime location and just temporarily empty while waiting for new tenants to move in. Or it may be in a shopping centre, clean and waiting for use.

More often, though, the shops used for pop ups are in side streets or just off the main high street, have been empty for some time and haven't been well maintained.

So the first sight of your shop is a slightly scruffy front, displaying the name of the last business that went bust, and some circus posters hanging inside the front door. One of the key benefits to a landlord is that you'll tidy up, make the shop look more inviting and make the unit easier to let in future.

You can restore a tatty shop front quite easily without major work, and it makes a huge difference to the experience you offer your visitors. Start by giving the shop a really good clean; you just need hot water, soap and some elbow grease! A window-cleaning squeegee is essential for windows. A mop is useful to get into higher spaces. Be prepared; you'll get wet, and the job is messy! Start at the top and work down, so you don't make a mess of areas you've already cleaned. (And yes, I know that sounds obvious, but it can be tempting to start with the easy bits, trust me!)

After you clean the shop front, you can evaluate whether you need to undertake any repairs or just apply a new coat of paint. You can see exactly how much work it'll take to brand your pop up shop front.

This checklist helps you decide how much time, effort and money to spend on the physical refurbishment of your shop front:

- ✔ Are the windows in good condition, and is the frame around them secure and not rotting? If the shop has large plate glass windows, do they feel well fixed? If you see rot or the windows feel loose, you need to replace some timber to make everything secure. Be careful! This job may be one for a specialist.

- ✔ On the inside, can you see evidence of water ingress, such as staining or water damage? If so, can you spot the leak, and is it an easy fix? If not, can you live with a little leak for the time you're open and simply be careful about what you place near it?

- ✔ Can you close and securely lock all windows and doors? If not, can you repair or replace them easily? Do you know exactly who has keys, or can you replace the barrels in locks while you're open?

Replace locks only with the agreement of the landlord or letting agent, as they may have rights to access the property – for example, to show it to prospective tenants.

- ✔ Do any security measures, such as wire grills over rear windows, protect vulnerable spots? If not, can you install them? Most hardware stores provide wire mesh in different thicknesses, which you can cut to fit and secure with screws and washers.

Signs

Signs are important. Look at the shops around yours; they more than likely have invested in clear signs, corporate identities and clever displays to make it comfortable for customers to come in and spend money.

The main sign above your shop may be your brand name or the name you're using for your pop up project. Alternatively, you may like the sign that's already there and keep it; many pop ups are very honest about their temporary nature and keep existing signs and shop fittings deliberately. Theatre Absolute runs a theatre in a former fish and chip restaurant in Coventry, and while the main frontage carries its branding, some signs inside still give away the shop's original use. One London gallery was based in a former bookmaker's shop, and the gallery kept the name City Racing. Margate's Pie Factory tells you exactly what the building used to be!

You can apply your branding in plenty of ways, to suit any budget:

- ✔ **Commission an artist to make you a sign on a board that you can fit over the existing shop sign.** If you commission an artist, give him a good brief but let him be creative; that's what artists are good at! An artist may be able to make extra items you need, such as A-boards (see next section) or interior signs.

- ✔ **Get commercial vinyl stickers made to apply in a blank space above the shop or on the shop's windows.** A local signmaker or printshop can print vinyls, and a single-colour design should be fairly cheap. Apply your own vinyls, which isn't too difficult with warm soapy water, a good eye and hard squeegee.

- ✔ **Paint over all existing signs so that your shop front is neutral.** Create temporary branding in the window display spaces only.

- ✔ **Use commercially printed PVC banners that you can move from one pop up project to the next.** You can hang these banners over any existing signs. In the Netherlands, many shops use such banners all year round.

Remember that a full commercial solution may be expensive for a short-term occupation and may not look very exciting either. So be creative, and bear in mind that a huge, home-made sign outside the venue may be more effective than a perfectly designed A4 poster in a window.

Many copy shops can enlarge an A4 black-and-white page to an A0 poster for just a few pounds. It's an easy way to turn artwork from a standard printer into something much more eye-catching. Be big, bold and colourful for the best effect.

Also remember to use signs and displays while you're preparing your shop space, as people become interested in what's happening. One shop in the Living Places project wrapped its windows in brown parcel paper to create a sense of excitement before it opened to the public.

A-boards

Putting signs on the street is an effective tool that you can use in a variety of ways. The most common type of sign is an *A-board*, which has two identical sides joined by a chain or rope to form an A-shape. But you can also get signs that spin or stand on a pedestal.

On a recent visit to Rotterdam, I was impressed by homemade A-boards created from recycled floorboards. In the past, I've made very simple A-boards from recycled wallpaper pasting tables.

Commercially available A-boards vary in price from around £25 to £250. You can have your custom designs printed on A-boards. A-boards can also be provided as blackboards (commonly seen outside cafes, for example) or can have a space covered by clear Perspex for you to display posters.

Placed at nearby junctions, A-boards can direct people to your shop, which is especially useful if you're in a secondary location. Directly outside your shop, A-boards can be a clear prompt to customers to come in. In both these cases, don't forget to make the directions to your pop up really clear by using arrows on your signs!

If your pop up has a programme of changing activity, such as performances or workshops, an A-board with a blackboard is a useful way to change information regularly.

Local byelaws may prohibit the use of A-boards and other street signs. Check with your local authority, but also scout the area and ask local shopkeepers. While such signs may be prohibited, the prohibition may be more honoured in the breach than the observance.

Street advertising

Some shops have an area between the shop front and the public pavement that actually belongs to the shop. You can usually tell, thanks to a difference in paving type. If you believe the pavement is public, check with your landlord or letting agent.

If you do have this area, think about how to use it. You can create an eye-catching display outside your shop or use simple planters to soften its appearance. Or you may find that this space becomes functional, with tables and chairs for your customers to sit and have a cup of tea.

Whatever you do, consider this area as part of your window display and use it to carry your branding to the street. Don't use it to park a car or store your bins!

Decorating Inside Your Shop

In art terms, the process of putting the displays together in a space is called *curating*. In retail, it's *merchandising*. Whatever you call it, the basic rule is the same: choose a style and stick to it. Find furniture and objects that match and treat the space as one big display.

Or if you're going to *zone* the interior – maybe a cafe area, a shop corner, a display space – use furniture and colours to make each area distinct.

Overall, you need to create an interior that looks smart and professional, but is functional and helps you achieve the aims of your pop up. Don't forget that whatever you do, it must help you get to the end point that you're after, not divert you from it!

Decoration

Many people are surprised at how scruffy the inside of an empty shop can look, which shows just how good the work of the army of designers, visual merchandisers and window dressers really is. Shops are functional workspaces, like factories for selling, and after you take away the pretty bits, you're left with a light industrial building!

The good news is that you can make any interior look great without major work, and it makes a huge difference to the experience you offer your visitors.

Start by giving the shop a really good clean. Just like cleaning the outside, you just need hot water, soap and the willingness to put in some hard work.

Recycle any rubbish and clear the shop of everything left behind by previous tenants that you can't use. Wash down work surfaces and counters, vacuum, and clean ancillary areas, such as toilets and storage space, too.

 Many shops smell damp; this odour is usually because they've been left sealed up while not in use, and not a sign of a major problem. Dehumidifiers make a difference. You can buy the most basic type, a small, plastic tub full of crystals that sits on a windowsill or surface, at hardware stores.

After you clean the shop, you can evaluate whether you need to undertake any repairs, whether it just needs a new coat of paint, and how you can brand the interior.

Ask yourself the following questions:

- ✔ Is the interior dry, or is water getting in somewhere?
- ✔ Is condensation a problem in any closed areas?
- ✔ Do interior doors and windows open, and can you secure them?

- ✔ Can you lock and secure an area – for example, a kitchen, storeroom or office – to provide a safe area for storing personal possessions?

- ✔ Do the electrics look safe? A visual inspection for any broken plug sockets and loose wires where lights have been removed is essential. Hire a professional tradesperson if you're uncertain about electrics or gas.

- ✔ Are all areas clear of rubbish and other possible hazards? (See Chapter 2 for more details about risk assessments.)

After the shop is clean and tidy, you may choose to decorate or simply touch up scruffy areas.

If some of your shop is painted and looks fresh and new, it can make the rest of it look even scruffier, and you may find you have to paint the whole shop! You can decorate yourself, but if you're not handy with a paint roller, hire somebody to decorate for you. Most shops are a fairly neutral space, so white emulsion is ideal just to freshen up.

In some shops, shabby chic may be a style you can work with, but don't start decorating until you're sure you want to go the whole way!

Colours

This book isn't about interior design, and I'm not Laurence Llewelyn-Bowen, but do consider using the key colours from your branding to add highlights or create features. (You can find out more about creating different areas in the 'Zones' section later in this chapter.)

Retail psychologists have studied the way colours work in shop spaces. At the most basic level, neutral colours can calm people, and vibrant colours can excite them. Light colours make spaces feel bigger, and deeper colours make them feel more intimate.

If you're going to paint, don't buy cheap emulsion: you'll use three times as much to get good coverage, and the time lost could be spent on other things. Similarly, really cheap brushes can be a false economy, as they shed bristles and you won't get a neat finish.

Lighting

After you've decorated, make sure that all the display lighting in the shop is working, and highlights the areas you want customers to focus on.

You may decide to replace or refurbish existing light fixtures. This task can be simple, for example replacing bulbs or changing a simple fitting that's broken. If it's more complicated, such as changing a whole range of fixtures, employ a qualified electrician.

If your shop still has dark and gloomy colours, consider using floor-standing lamps, table lamps or angle-poise lamps in different places to brighten up the shop. You can buy small clip-on spotlights quite cheaply to create a dramatic effect.

Branding

You can find much more about how to create your branding in Chapter 6, but in this section I look at how to bring your branding (which is usually a two-dimensional logo and set of colours) into a three-dimensional space.

The aim of using your branding in your pop up is to emphasise the key elements of your brand without hitting your customers over the head repeatedly with one logo!

Think about how big supermarkets use a combination of colours, consistent fonts and logo shapes to apply their branding across the store. You encounter the store's branding on signs outside, on shelf edges and point-of-sale signs throughout the shop, and it's on your receipt and plastic bag as you leave, so you even take it home with you.

Or think about how art galleries use signs. When you walk into a room at any of the four Tate galleries, you know exactly where you are, and a sign tells you what the room's about in big, clear letters. Individual rooms can show radically different art, yet the consistent signs keep you moving and comfortable throughout your visit.

So you use whatever fonts you've settled on for your branding consistently across your pop up. Restrict your fonts to one or two, no more. Think about how you can apply the fonts from your brand style to everything, from price tags to posters. You can spend your budget getting these commercially printed or take a more creative approach by using stencils and rubber stamps.

Think about how you can use the colours of your brand in decorating your pop up. If you colour match a feature wall, some furniture or even just hang bold fabric that's the same colour, you'll reinforce your brand.

If you're using social media, you have an online brand to build as well (see Chapter 8). Think about ways to link your pop up and the online audience. For example, if you use a hashtag on Twitter, display it clearly on signs in your shop so that people know to use it.

We Are Bedford was a community project that used a series of pop up projects to bring life to the deserted Castle Quay area of the town. Over the space of a few months, the project brought the area back to life and increased the occupancy of shop units. As the project kept moving from one place and one project to another, a strong brand was a vital ingredient in building recognition and keeping an audience engaged. The We Are Bedford logo used a cut-out font that was applied to window vinyls, laser-cut signs and a rubber stamp to create hanging tags and paper bags. A stencil was cut to quickly spray paint the logo on walls and furniture. The logo was flexible and adaptable to lots of different uses in the various pop ups, and the cut-out font could be copied easily for use on blackboards, too.

Design clear signs explaining what the project is about. Again, enlarge it at a copy shop for legibility. If you use your signs to explain the temporary nature of the project, it can attract people who want to get involved in this or future projects; and it can calm nervous visitors who don't understand your project.

Whatever form your branding takes, when it comes to the inside of your pop up, apply it in a way that's:

- ✔ Clear
- ✔ Creative
- ✔ Consistent

And don't forget, your branded elements must be demountable – you need to clear it all away when you leave so that the shop returns to an empty, unbranded shell ready for future tenants.

Window displays

Your shop window is a vital part of your branding and sells your pop up to passers-by. It needs to be individual and eye-grabbing, but also explain what your pop up's all about in visual terms. In short, it's a piece of shop-front storytelling.

The technical term for shop displays is *visual merchandising*. Knowing the proper name is helpful, but it's also worth remembering that creating displays is exactly what you're doing!

Fight the urge to put a big stack of your product right in the window. I saw one shop in Margate that had window displays of stacked-up toilet roll and lines of washing up liquid bottles. While it said exactly what the shop did, it wasn't that enticing! Conveying the spirit of your pop up is more important than showing off every product. This advice is particularly true if you have lots of people's products in your pop up – for example, if you're running a gallery for a collective of artists.

Always bear in mind the aim of your pop up (Chapter 2) and your branding (Chapter 6). You need to get those ideas across in objects. You can use your favourite product, well displayed, or a prop that sums up what you do. You can create a themed display; I used old suitcases stacked up to say 'travel' in a pop up tourist information centre, for example. Likewise, AllSaints has displayed Singer sewing machines in its windows to say, 'We make clothes'. (Incidentally, these displays have driven the price of an old Singer sewing machine up by 300 per cent!)

Here are a few more tips for making your window displays pop:

- ✔ **Use a backdrop to separate the window from the shop.** This backdrop doesn't have to be solid; it can just be a freestanding screen or a hanging cloth. But a backdrop makes your window display stand out more clearly by separating it from the visual clutter in the shop behind it.

- ✔ **Make maximum use of the height and depth of your window.** By displaying products or props at different heights, you catch the eye of people at different places in the street. Use purpose-built plinths or stacks of boxes to create different heights and levels or suspend items using clear nylon fishing line.

- ✔ **Consider the size of the products you're displaying.** If they're small, using a plinth and a backdrop may help give them a big visual impact if they're seen from further away. If they're large, use just one or two and they'll have a big impact!

- ✔ **Use lighting to make your products or props stand out even more.** Many windows have built-in spotlights, but if not, you can use clip-on spotlights or even angle-poise lamps effectively.

However you approach your windows, try to:

- ✔ Keep it simple.
- ✔ Clean your windows and the shelves inside.
- ✔ Use colour and pattern, with care.

Stock displays

Everything you've considered for your window displays (see preceding section) applies equally to the displays you create inside the pop up. Here, though, you need to mix the big visual impact with the display of a wider range of products.

If you're opening a pop up, you probably don't want to spend your budget on expensive shop fittings that you'll use only for a short time. Shops like IKEA are great sources of affordable, funky furniture.

Even better than buying new furniture is recycling; embrace the temporary nature of the project and find furniture for free, using your local Freegle group. You can recycle, restore and remake found furniture, fixtures and fittings to create high-impact interior designs.

Give secondhand furniture a lick of paint. Everything painted white looks stylish and professional, or if you fancy more fun try mis-matched primary colours. Painted and then sanded back can create an upmarket, slightly bohemian air, while high-gloss paint can look modern and streetwise. Of course, with new or secondhand furniture, you could paint in your corporate colours or find ways to apply your branding to it.

Or pick a style and source furniture from local junk shops, charity stores, car boot sales and flea markets. A 1950s-styled cafe with plastic tables or a fashion boutique filled with vintage wardrobes are great examples.

You can often borrow what you need, too:

- ✔ Friends and colleagues may be able to help out with loans for a short-term pop up.

- ✔ Larger local stores may also be able to help with the loan of shopfittings, shelving and so on.

- ✔ Local community centres, charities and organisations may be able to loan you other things that you need, such as tables and chairs.

Don't be afraid to create display equipment that plays on the temporary nature of the project. You can screw together old rough wooden pallets to make shelves and display stands. Scaffolding can make temporary structures. Battered wooden stepladders can create bold display shelves for products.

However you furnish your interior, remember that it must be functional, match your brand and meet the aims of your pop up.

Zones

In the perfect world, you'd have staff to greet each customer at the door, guide them through the shop and help them make purchases, but, of course, that's not realistic. But good store design guides customers, informs them, entertains them along the way and ultimately helps them make purchases or get involved in other activities. Think about how the zones within your shop can help your customers use the shop, and as a consequence, help you achieve your aims.

Think carefully about how your space will work. A big, open space with large windows may make a great gallery space, but may be intimidating for visitors if you're running workshops and they feel they're being watched. Can you create multiple spaces in your shop – a quiet corner for meetings and workshops, a wider space for displaying art or products and an office area out the back?

One key space in your shop is the *transition zone* – the area immediately inside the door, where customers who walk in work out where to go and what to do. The transition zone is a space where people need to adjust to the lighting, the displays and all the other stuff they can see. You'll see people slow down or even stop near the door. Ever walked into a shop and had to go back to the door to pick up a basket? That's because the baskets were in the transition zone, and you were still adjusting!

Stand in the transition zone, just inside your door, and look around:

✔ Can you see clearly what the shop is and what it does?

✔ Can you move furniture or displays so that they're clearly visible from the transition zone and use them to draw people further in?

✔ Is your branding clearly visible, along with prompts to take action, such as tweeting about your pop up?

Understanding the layout of your shop is really important, and making that visible from the door is a good start.

Now think about the other zones you may need. These zones are specific to things you need to do in your pop up, so they're tailored to your specific project. Here are some examples:

- ✔ Art gallery
    - Gallery area
    - Sales desk
    - Wrapping area for valuable/fragile goods
    - Tea/coffee area for charming high-end buyers
    - Storage for paintings and sculptures not on show
- ✔ Fashion boutique
    - Display areas
    - Changing room
    - Sales desk with room for folding clothes
- ✔ Community space
    - Workshop area
    - Workspace for admin
    - Tea/coffee area
    - Cafe seating
- ✔ Cafe
    - Kitchen/food preparation area
    - Main area with tables and chairs
    - Reception ᵣᵤd cash desk

When laying out the zones, remember that ideally you want to guide people to the back of the shop. The aim is to make them engage with your brand or spend money – and the longer they're in the shop, the more chance you'll have to achieve this goal. That's why supermarkets put the essentials, such as bread and milk, at the back and in the centre of their store; it means you have to get deep into the store, and then they can catch you with impulse buys.

Your shoppers are called *visitors*. If you count the number of visitors to your shop and the number of time your till rings, you can work out the *conversion rate*. If you have ten customers and five purchases, you have a 50 per cent conversion. The time people spend in your shop is called *dwell time*. So you can measure *visitors*, *dwell* and *conversion* to work out exactly how your shop works! Of course, for a pop up, these numbers are much harder to measure, but it's well worth keeping some record of total number of visitors, the time they spend in each zone and your total sales.

Footfall Counters (www.footfallcounters.com) have a range of counters that use infra-red technology to measure how many people walk through your door. These easy-to-install mobile devices automatically count the footfall both overall and by zone, with prices from £69. However, they do count repeat visitors and your staff, too. A handheld counter or a tally sheet behind your till are adequate for up to a few hundred visitors a day, and you can adjust it to not count repeat visits.

Chapter 11

Managing Your Shop and Staff

In This Chapter

▶ Putting up the 'Open' sign

▶ Organising your team

▶ Keeping track of stock and sales

*I*f you want an easy life, you need to put the right systems in place to ensure that your shop works. Ever been to a cafe and watched the staff struggle to give the right people the right drinks? A cafe is easy to run, as long as you have the right systems in place. A pop up is no different.

In this chapter, I look at some of the systems you can have in place to make your pop up run smoothly. I assume that you're running some kind of shop. If you're running a specialised pop up, such as a cinema, restaurant, park or something even more unusual, you need to develop more specialist systems. But the basic systems I describe in this chapter should help with that process.

Deciding on Your Opening Times

Making sure that your pop up is open at the right time is for fairly obvious reasons very important, but this detail is often overlooked.

If your opening times are right, you'll be able to attract the highest number of visitors, in the shortest possible time. This means the highest profit at the lowest cost, of course.

Choosing set opening times and displaying them clearly in the window is vital. Don't try to be clever; put a very clear list of opening days and times in the window, either hung up as a poster or by using printed vinyl stickers applied to the window. Nothing's more disappointing for a pop up fan than turning up at an event to discover that it's closed. Put the same information on your website.

Choosing opening times

Only you can choose the opening times for your pop up, but here are some details to guide you:

- ✓ **Work out at what times your target audience can or cannot come to your pop up.** For example, if you're targeting young people, opening only during school hours limits the success of your pop up.

- ✓ **Look at local patterns of footfall.** Your town centre manager may be able to provide *footfall data*, the statistical analysis of when customers use the town centre. If the town centre manager can't help you, visit the location of your pop up at different times to gather some anecdotal evidence.

- ✓ **Identify peaks in footfall, such as on market days or during a local arts festival.** Match your opening times to those increases, but be aware that they may not automatically bring *you* more visitors.

You're better off advertising that you're open for fewer hours and getting the highest number of visitors in the shortest time. Being open for more hours doesn't mean you'll get more visitors.

For the Artists and Makers Festival, artists opened their homes and studios to art lovers. In the early years, artists tried opening all week. It was hard work, and visitor numbers were slow but steady throughout the week. In subsequent years, the festival chose to open only on weekends; the same number of visitors came, but all in a shorter time. The open houses felt busier and the staffing costs were reduced.

Some pop ups are open for one evening only, forcing all their visitors into a short space of time and making sure that their shop is bursting at the seams. This plan can work really well, but it's a high-risk strategy. What happens if your short opening time coincides with a thunderstorm? Or even worse, somebody else throws an even better party just round the corner?

Matching local events

Local factors have an impact on footfall to a local area. Look for listings online, but also contact tourist information centres to ask for their inside knowledge.

Local events which may have an effect on your footfall include:

- ✔ Arts, food and music festivals
- ✔ Market days
- ✔ Sports matches and events
- ✔ Late-night shopping or seasonal shopping events

An increase in local footfall doesn't necessarily mean a rise in visitors to your event. People who've come to a place for one event may not want (or have time) to visit another.

Developing Systems

Putting systems in place means that your shop can run smoothly, but also that you'll have less work to do because your team knows what's happening, what goes where and how to deal with things that happen.

Insisting on systems may seem like you're trying to take control, but what you're really doing is giving your team the control to do what it wants and needs to do, without your pop up running into problems.

Think about how different people may use your pop up so that you can identify the systems you need to create. Consider the perspectives of:

 ✔ Your partners in the pop up.

 ✔ The members of your team.

 ✔ People visiting your pop up.

You won't be able to anticipate everything, but you should be able to identify the key systems.

Daily social media

Social media needs to be a part of the working life of your pop up. Using social media as you go about your business means that it's easy to manage and delivers real engagement with your pop up.

In Chapter 8, I look at how to create a message grid. Make this grid available in your shop, with a note of key messages. Encourage staff to use this message grid to spread your message through their own social media channels.

Think about how to use different channels in the day-to-day running of your pop up:

 ✔ Post regular status updates on your Facebook page. Monitor the site for live customer feedback.

 ✔ Add images from your pop up to Flickr and encourage visitors who take photographs to add them to your Flickr group, too. Include photos of your decor, products and customers.

 ✔ Upload short clips to YouTube or Vimeo. Include footage of your shop at its busiest.

Staff identification

A small step toward making using your pop up easy for customers is to help them clearly identify your staff members.

You probably don't want to go as far as McDonald's, with a uniform and name badge. But if your staff are dressed in completely casual clothes, it can be hard for customers to find them when they need them.

Find some way to identify your staff:

- ✔ Give them name badges.
- ✔ Print T-shirts with your logo or a slogan.
- ✔ Ask them to wear colour-coded dress.
- ✔ Have branded lanyards produced.

A pop up food stall that appears among the burger stands at music festivals has found a bold way to make its staff stand out. Strumpets with Crumpets sells exactly what the title suggests: crumpets from Lakeland Bake in Cumbria with a variety of top-pings. The staff are exactly what you'd expect, too: in character as slightly burlesque ladies in corsets, feathers and fur.

Sales process

You must carefully monitor sales, particularly where multiple partners are involved in the pop up, such as a shop shared by artists and makers.

Producing a clear sales sheet at the end of the pop up is essential, to set out your opening stock, any sales and what stock is left at the end. To produce this sales sheet:

1. **Count and record all stock before you open.**

2. **Record all sales and any losses through damage while you're open.**

3. **Count closing stock, which should equal the amount of all the items from point 1 minus those from point 2.**

Stock control

Stock control systems can cost you hundreds of thousands, with complicated computer systems, bar codes and warehouses. Most pop ups don't have anything near that complicated.

All the most simple or the most complicated stock control system does is record:

- ✔ What items you have.
- ✔ How many items exist.
- ✔ The wholesale and the retail price of each item.
- ✔ Where the stock is stored.

The most effective way to control stock for a pop up is probably the simplest. Create a document with four columns. Fill these in as stock is delivered to the pop up (see Table 11-1).

Table 11-1	A Stock Control Document			
Item	*Quantity*	*Wholesale Cost*	*Retail Price*	*Stored*
She Makes War CD	10	£5	£10	Shelf 1
Mocking Kevin CD	5	£3	£8	Shelf 2

Sales records

You need to record all sales. You may opt to use a bar code system or a till that records sales automatically.

If not, and if you're managing sales for a number of partners, you need to record all sales to ensure that you can balance your stock against your sales.

To record sales for your pop up, create a document with four columns (see Table 11-2) and keep a copy on your sales desk.

Table 11-2	A Document for Recording Sales		
Item	*Artist*	*Quantity*	*Total price*
Kitesurfing painting	Tracey Thompson	1	£450
Landscape drawing	Debbie Zoutewelle	2 x £30 each	£60
Photo	Nathan Bean	1	£300

Accounts

In this book, I don't look at accounting in great detail, as I'm assuming that your pop up is part of a larger business or you're self-employed, and because of that, you have established accounting systems in place.

As part of the day-to-day running of your pop up, however, have some basic accounting systems in place. You need:

- ✔ **Petty cash** to cover running expenses, such as toilet paper and teabags. Create a simple system to record how it's used, such as an envelope for receipts.

- ✔ **Float** in your till, to provide change when customers make purchases.

- ✔ **To bank your takings** at the end of each day, probably not in a bank but in a secure location, ready for banking at the end of your pop up.

At the end of your pop up, create a daily sheet that records petty cash, what it was spent on and the total sales from your pop up that day.

I cover more on bookkeeping in Chapter 4.

Enquiries

Your pop up may generate leads that you need to follow up. The impact of your pop up carries on long after you've packed up, closed the doors and gone back to what you were doing before.

The leads may be new customers or better relationships with existing customers. These may have opened opportunities for future sales. When you're selling high-value items, customers may well want to spend some time considering before making a purchase.

Leads may be media enquiries or related to new media, such as requests for further information from bloggers. Or you may attract enquiries for your partners or interest in your venue, and you need to pass these on promptly.

Keep a notebook by your sales desk and record all enquiries. Make sure that your team members know where the notebook is and that they need to record names and contact details alongside the enquiry. Of course, you could use a laptop, but if you do, all staff members need to be able to access it at all times.

Work through these leads in the week after your pop up, and make sure everyone receives a response from you, even if it's only to say that you've passed the details to somebody else who can help.

Stock rooms

Keeping track of stock is important, particularly if you have many partners in your pop up.

Pop ups with complicated stock control may include a group of artists working together or a food co-op where many producers are selling their products.

In any case, stock rooms need to be secure and stock managed. It may be that you're using a space, such as an empty shop or a church hall, where such a space physically exists. If not, you may need to use a shop counter, tables or screens to create a stock area that only your staff can access. You can use locked cupboards to secure stock. You can design these cupboards into your pop up as part of your kit out.

You may also need some controls over the movement of goods from your stock room to where they're sold. For example, you may not want too many staff moving stock because it can become tricky to monitor where everything is.

In pop ups with many users – for example, a collection of people producing locally made goods – the stock room is probably best managed by giving each trader their own defined area and labelling these spaces. Make sure that all stock is recorded as it's delivered so that you can balance stock at the end of the pop up.

Health and safety

Managing the risks and the health and safety requirements of a pop up largely comes down to common sense and being careful without being overly cautious.

Risk assessment isn't static and as you now have the keys to your shop, you can carry out a more detailed assessment.

After this assessment, you need to make sure that everybody working in your pop up is briefed about the risks and how you're managing them. You can make everyone aware through an informal induction as people come to the space for the first time – much the same as welcoming someone to your house and saying 'mind the step as you come in'.

Keep a copy of the complete risk assessment in the shop, clearly labelled, for people to refer to if they want to. Be prepared to update it if new risks are identified.

Daily checks

In Chapter 2, I break the risks down into three areas:

- ✔ Fire safety
- ✔ Health and safety
- ✔ Security

Break the risks down into these three areas and use these checklists for your own risk assessment:

Fire safety checklist:

- ✔ Have a phone available to make emergency calls.
- ✔ Clear away rubbish and safely store other materials and resources.
- ✔ Mark fire exits and clear routes of obstructions.
- ✔ Test any alarms and equipment.
- ✔ Have an evacuation plan in place and inform all staff and volunteers.

Health and safety:

- ✔ Have a phone available to make emergency calls.

- ✔ Ensure that public areas are clean, tidy and free of hazards (for example, trip hazards or stacked boxes).

- ✔ Close and clearly mark areas that are off limit to the public.

- ✔ Make sure that electrics and any portable electrical items are safe and visually check them for damage or broken cables.

- ✔ Only let staff and volunteers use any specialised equipment.

Security:

- ✔ Have a phone available to make emergency calls.

- ✔ Close and lock windows and doors when the premises are not in use.

- ✔ Lock and secure doors and windows in unused areas.

- ✔ Offer a safe, locked area for private possessions, such as bags and coats.

Keys and keyholders

For security, you need to manage who has keys and can access your pop up. Ideally, you need two or three keyholders. Create a simple rota to decide who opens and closes the shop each day. On closing the pop up, ensure the keyholder checks that:

- ✔ Nobody is left in your pop up, including in the toilet, staff room, stock room and so on.

- ✔ All windows and doors are closed, locked and secured.

- ✔ Fire exits are left clear.

- ✔ All electrical items are safe, with equipment like kettles and coffee machines switched off.

Backstage

Stock rooms, kitchen areas, unused spaces and toilets are all the *backstage* of your pop up.

The backstage areas need less management than the front-of-houses areas, the parts seen by your customers. However, they need to be tidy, safe and secure so that customers can't wander into them by mistake.

Staff

Managing staff can seem intimidating. Whether they're friends you're sharing the space with, a team pulled together from partner organisations, volunteers keen to support your cause or people you're directly employing, putting systems in place makes your job easier.

Timetables

Draw up clear timetables of all the times your pop up needs staff. Include the times when you're:

- ✔ Setting up and fitting out.
- ✔ Preparing to open each day.
- ✔ Open to customers.
- ✔ Closing, tidying and restocking each day.
- ✔ Packing up.
- ✔ Making the space ready to return keys.

You need to decide which staff are needed at which times. Be aware that at certain times you'll need extra staff – for example, you may well be very busy in the final few hours of setting up, just before you open, or need extra staff at an opening party. Remember to make sure that a keyholder is available for opening and closing each day.

After you have a timetable, create a blank table (your *staff roster*) and fill in which staff will do which shifts. Then follow this checklist:

- ✔ Make sure that all staff members agree to the shifts you assign.
- ✔ Give them all a copy of the final, agreed roster.
- ✔ Keep a copy of the staff roster in the pop up for reference.
- ✔ Remind staff members when they're due in next.

Staff problems

Employing temporary staff means that both you and they have rights and responsibilities (see Chapter 3). Whether your staff members are employed on fixed-term contracts, as freelancers or as volunteers, be clear with them about what they're expected to do and the hours they're expected to work.

During a pop up, things can be fast and furious. Everyone involved is putting in a massive amount of energy, often working long hours to make everything happen on time. Often, people have made an emotional commitment, too, because they're very involved in the cause, message or aim of the pop up.

In many ways, a pop up is less like running a shop, and more like putting on a stage play. At times, people are tired and egos clash, and you have to deal with staff problems.

These clashes are normal. When they happen, let people have their say without allocating any blame. Let them get it out of their system, but backstage and not in front of customers!

Accept responsibility but don't take it personally. Identify the problem and take whatever action is needed to keep the pop up running. At the end of the day, 'the show's the thing'!

Chapter 12

Meeting Your Customers

. . . .

In This Chapter

▶ Meeting and greeting visitors

▶ Fostering relationships with future customers

. . . .

You've done all the hard work, and now you're ready to open your shop and meet the customers. No matter what the aim of your pop up, the actual *point* of it is this time you're going to spend with the public!

If you're running a pop up by yourself or with a very small team, meeting your customers can be especially difficult. After the planning and the frantic fit out, you'll be feeling worn out, and finding the energy to be bright, cheerful and chatty can be hard.

But now you're open and you've got a top team around you, it's your job to ensure that your pop up keeps doing exactly what it's supposed to do.

Chapter 11 covers putting systems in place to make sure that your pop up runs like a well-oiled machine. This chapter is all about meeting your customers and giving them the best experience possible.

Engaging your customers is the fun bit. It's when your ideas really come to life. If you're testing something new, then this is nail-biting stuff. If you're offering a treat for valued customers, you're catching up with old friends. If your pop up is theatrical, it's showtime. Whatever it is you're doing, now's the critical moment.

Using social media during the day

Use the social media you're signed up with to let people know when you're open. Start with a message each day that says something like 'Just opened the pop up for day three' and send a few reminders during the day to catch people who log on at different times. Most importantly, tweet about what's happening. Commenting on who's in the shop and what's selling well, and highlighting products that have nearly sold out all help to create a buzz around your brand.

Shops in the Seven Dials area of London may have their own Twitter accounts, but one also exists for the whole area, @7DialsWC2. The account regularly announces that new pop ups have opened, reminds followers what shops are already in the area and highlights special offers. It also mentions some celebrity shoppers spotted in the neighbourhood. Most importantly, it opens conversations with people who mention the area, inviting them in to local shops.

Meeting and Greeting While You're Open

Whenever you go to a McDonald's, anywhere, you get the same service. The staff behind the counter work from the same script, and when your food's served, it looks exactly the same as the last time you ate there. While McDonald's customers like that guarantee of a set standard, it can be a little bit soulless. If you're in a strange town, hearing an unfamiliar dialect and tasting something new is more exciting.

Your pop up may aim to deliver a set standard for every customer, but should probably be a bit more cheerful, uplifting and interesting than a visit to a fast food chain.

Briefing staff

Although a staff briefing may seem rather formal, it's worth getting your team together briefly each time for ten minutes just before you open. This briefing doesn't need to be a formal meeting; you can just start the day by gathering everybody together, making them a cup of tea and having a few quick words while you share the biscuits out!

If you have different staff at different times while you're open, then this briefing is essential. You need to brief your team on the systems you have for running the shop and on any health and safety stuff they need to know.

Although you can tell people individually, getting everyone together saves time and helps build a little team spirit. Bringing your team members together regularly reminds them that they're all on the same side and working toward a common aim. Make sure you keep reminding people exactly why they're there and make the aim of your pop up really clear.

Set a slightly different target to strive for each day, to get your staff more involved in your pop up. For example, the target could be to get the highest daily sales figure, or the most items bought in a single sale. Or something more fun – like finding out an unusual fact about every customer as you talk to them. The target can help you achieve your overall aim. This motivates, enthuses and directs your team's energy. It works for you too!

Letting people know you're open

The 'Open' sign that hangs in your shop's doorway is one of your most important bits of kit! Make sure that you buy one or, better yet, custom make one that reflects your pop up's branding.

In Chapter 10, I write about the transition zone immediately inside the door of your shop. Another un-named zone is even more crucial. The pavement immediately outside your shop is an important bit of property. It's where people choose to visit your shop . . . or not.

Most shops ignore this space, but it's vital. You need to use your pavement transition zone to make it very clear to pass- ersby that you're open and to invite them to step into your shop. Spend some time in a local street and watch how many people hover outside a shop without going in; these are lost customers!

Bigger shops keep their front doors wide open the whole time they're open, or they have automatic doors that open when you're close and invite you to step inside. (Yes, automatic doors aren't just there for lazy people; they help you step over the threshold!)

Open doors obviously help, but they're not very practical if it's cold, windy or raining, or if you have goods on display that bad weather may damage. In those situations, consider doing something else to let customers know you're open. Remember, you're a pop up, and that means you're fresh, urgent and exciting, so get that message out on the street!

To make it obvious you're open, consider:

- ✔ **Bunting, flags or balloons** to tell people exactly where you are; they're like an urban shorthand that says something exciting is happening. You can purchase these items in your corporate branding colours. You may even want to hire a local artist to make custom-made designs or have a commercial printer make you a custom-made alternative with your branding on it.

- ✔ **Planters and plant-pots** as a simple way to extend your shop onto the pavement; they're colourful, friendly and welcoming. Remember to water them and bring them inside when you close at night.

- ✔ **Seats and benches** which are used by many cafes and restaurants. Shopping is increasingly a social activity, so giving passersby a spot to stop and be sociable right outside your shop isn't a bad idea!

- ✔ **A-boards and swinging signs** on the street, as an effective way to say that you're open and tell passersby about any activities, such as talks and workshops in your pop up. However, these signs are so commonplace that they're easy to ignore. If you use them, make sure that they're interesting and eye-catching.

Local bylaws may prohibit the use of A-boards, street signs and furniture outside your shop. Check with your local authority, but also scout the area and ask local shopkeepers. See Chapter 10 for more about signs and regulations.

On the days you're open, you can also use signs on street corners to direct people your way. Find out whether any sites are nearby where you can legally hang a temporary banner or signpost. And if you can display an A-board, put one out in a prominent location.

Engaging customers

Your pop up has all gone according to plan. You're open, the shop looks fabulous and, even better, you have customers coming in through the door. What can go wrong now?

Well, you can completely fail to engage with those customers. Ever walked into a shop and not felt welcome? If you have, you probably won't go back to that shop in a hurry. After you've lost a customer, winning them back again is very hard.

Making visitors feel welcome

Aim to make all the visitors to your pop up feel welcome, without being too pushy. High-pressure sales won't work in a pop up, so don't worry about the hard sell.

You also don't have the chance to really get to know regular customers, either, like you would in a shop that's around for longer, so you need to build relationships quickly.

Start with the basics, but don't be overpowering. A polite 'hello' as people come in always works. And this point is obvious: make eye contact and remember to smile!

You may feel so comfortable in the space you've created, particularly if you've been working with just a small team, that you start to treat it like home. Don't!

In addition:

- ✔ Don't ignore people when they come in.
- ✔ Don't huddle with friends or colleagues in deep conversation.
- ✔ Don't bury your head in a book.
- ✔ Don't eat food at your shop counter.

The best shop staff are the ones who are interested in and enthusiastic about what they're doing. To create the best experience for customers, staff need to be:

- ✔ **Prompt.** You need to stop whatever you're doing to help customers and serve them. Everything else – phone calls, sorting out stock and drinking coffee – comes second to the customer who's in front of you.

- ✔ **Friendly.** It feels awkward for this British author, but the Americans have it right: 'how are you' and 'have a nice day' go a long way. Polite but relaxed conversation is important to engage customers.

- ✔ **Listening.** Hear what your customers say, respond to them and adjust your pop up to answer any recurring questions. The customer may not always be right (see Chapter 6), but you always need to listen to them!

- ✔ **Willing to go further.** Service is something that sets you apart from the competition. Encourage your staff to give the extra inch and let customers take the extra mile. A cup of coffee, a free postcard or gift-wrapping are simple enough but make customers feel special.

Spreading word about your brand

While you're engaging with customers, make sure that they're linked to your whole brand and not just the pop up. Make sure that they can take away your details, too, by giving them postcards, business cards or a simple leaflet.

In addition, tell them all the ways in which they can keep engaged with your brand. If you have a Facebook group or fan page, a YouTube channel or a Flickr group, put the address on posters or vinyls around the shop.

Similarly, if you're using a hashtag on Twitter, tell people what it is by writing it on the wall. To create the maximum engagement, use a projector or display on a screen a real-time display of all the tweets using your hashtag. A number of websites can help you create a display:

- ✔ http://twitterfall.com/: Creates a stream of tweets and can be customised to show an account, hashtag or many other configurations.

- ✔ http://visibletweets.com: A more animated version, creating interesting visuals from tweets.

Engaging with customers who aren't in the shop

Social media has given people a way to engage with potential customers who aren't even in the shop. Make sure that you have WiFi or mobile connectivity when you're in the shop or have somebody monitoring social media on your behalf. While you're open, search by hashtag and by keywords relevant to your geographical location, too.

Respond to comments that mention your shop, even if the customers are some physical distance away and won't be visiting; they may have friends or followers more locally!

With more technical knowledge, you can make a custom display using RSS feeds from `www.twitter.com`.

If you're planning future events, make sure you give your customers details before they leave. A simple flyer is a good reminder.

Counting visitors

One of the key indicators of the success of your pop up is the number of customers. This number may not necessarily be a high target; for some high-end products, you may only want to invite a few carefully chosen people.

Shoe manufacturer Converse created a pop up in central London. The number of customers wasn't important; in fact, general customers weren't welcome. Kitted out as working offices with a reception area, the entire pop up was designed to show off the next year's Converse range to prospective retail buyers.

As another example, painter Adrian Crick creates the most intimate pop up, when he opens a bi-annual art gallery in his front room. It's not open to the public, but is an invite-only event for his mailing list of regular buyers and collectors.

Whether you're after a large number of visitors or a very select few, you'll need to keep a record of visitor numbers.

Create a tally sheet. Break the times you're open into shifts, such as morning, lunchtime and afternoon. Record the number of visitors during each shift. Also, record the total value of sales during each shift. (This number can be a rough amount; you don't need a complete breakdown in these figures.)

You can now identify your most successful periods when open. If you're really agile, you can even adjust staff levels accordingly so that you can ensure that your customers always get the best experience! You can also use this information to measure not only the success of your pop up, but also to inform future pop ups (see Chapter 13).

If you have huge numbers of visitors or you're open for weeks on end, it may not be possible to count everyone in and out. Count visitors for an hour a day, multiply by the number of hours you're open and use this number to estimate footfall.

Following Up and Attracting Future Customers

Your pop up may be a chance to catch up with valued and trusted customers, or it may be about building a longer, deeper and more meaningful relationship between them and your brand. Or perhaps your pop up is about meeting possible future customers and starting new relationships.

In either case, capturing useful information and using it to keep in touch is absolutely vital. A few years ago, getting a postal address counted as a good result. Nowadays, the cost of physical mailing is probably too high to make that approach worthwhile. Instead, you need to ask for an email address so that you can send them regular, targeted emails.

But even email is looking old-fashioned now; Likes on Facebook and followers on Twitter have increasingly replaced direct emailing.

Love us or hate us?

Love us or hate us? That's the question Marmite asked when it opened its pop up.

The yeast extract is well known for being loved or hated, and the brand has learned to play on that strong reaction to build presence and recognition.

The first Marmite pop up store opened on Regent Street, one of London's most sought after locations. The shop then popped up four more times, in locations around the world, in the following two years.

The first 1,000-square-foot shop included a cafe that not only sold Marmite, but Marmite-inspired art, books and merchandise. The shop was heavily branded, featured Marmite's yellow colour and used handwritten signs and quirky displays to make it feel like an independent shop.

The five pop ups attracted more than 500,000 visitors, and over 70,000 products were sold.

The Times, Guardian, Evening Standard, Sky News and Independent all wrote about the first pop up, and they all created blog, Facebook and Twitter posts.

More importantly, the pop up allowed visitors to engage with the Marmite brand. They could buy both 'I love . . .' and 'I hate . . .' merchandise. In the cafe, they could graffiti on the table with permanent markers, and messages were split between the lovers and haters. Customers could sign a giant guest book. Finally, customers could vote on a wall by adding Marmite stickers to large 'I love' or 'I hate' signs.

As well as capturing email addresses, the pop up created a sizeable following for the brand on Facebook and Twitter. Some customers were so fired up that they even started a petition to make the shop permanent and handed it over with hundreds of names and email addresses! It didn't become permanent but remained one of the most fondly remembered pop ups of all time.

Capturing customer information

Find as many ways as possible to capture useful information from your customers when they visit your pop up:

✔ **Ask them to leave their email address so that you can add them to your own mailing list.** You can use a form on the counter, postcards dropped around the shop or a working computer in the store.

✔ **Use a visitors' book to capture both email addresses and comments from visitors.** Ideally, place the book near the door so that it's visible as customers leave. A visitors' book is particularly appropriate for art galleries and other creative pop ups.

✔ **Be inspired and get interactive.** A big board, sticky notes and a pen provide a far more visually exciting way to encourage feedback.

✔ **Offer as many opportunities to interact on social media as possible.** Use signs linking to Facebook groups and show relevant hashtags throughout your pop up.

Consider how you can offer visitors an incentive to give you their details. You can enter them into a prize draw, offer a discount or give some other perk for volunteering their information.

In the UK, the data you collect may be covered by the Data Protection Act. In the United States, the Federal Trade Commission regulates how businesses collect, use and secure their customers' personal information. Make sure that you comply with relevant laws when you collect and share customer data.

Recording information for strategic partners

If you're working with a range of partners (see Chapter 3), they may want you to collect and share certain data.

With funding, you'll find that application forms expect you to collect certain information, such as visitor numbers. When drawing up partnership agreements, even if they're informal, be clear about what information will be collected and who it will be shared with.

While collecting information is important, don't let this process compromise the friendly and informal nature of your empty shops project. Don't let collecting information become more important than achieving the original aim of your pop up.

Keeping in touch

As a child, I'd go on holiday and make new friends. For a month or so after the holiday, I'd keep in touch with phone calls and letters, but the friendship would always fizzle out. Well, there's no excuse for that now, thanks to social media.

After you make friends, you need to keep in touch with them. You can find much more detail about using social media in Chapter 8, and the main reason for it is to keep up the engagement with your customers.

Consider whether you could email, message or tweet them in the week after your pop up, thanking them for visiting. This process may be time consuming, so consider sorting your friends and followers into lists.

Google Alerts

Not all your customers will be in direct contact with you, but Google and other search engines are all about helping you to find them. Google Alerts at www.google.com/alerts is particularly useful because it sends you a notification when new content is found.

You can set up searches for anything: your business name, the place where you're opening a pop up or keywords relating to what your pop up does. You can also choose how often you receive alerts, and they'll be mailed directly to your inbox.

Twitter searches

How you search Twitter depends on how you manage it. While you can search the website itself at any time, you can also use decks to create automated searches (see Chapter 8). However you choose to use Twitter, use searches to identify and then maintain engagement with visitors to your pop up.

Facebook Pages

Facebook Pages create a perfect platform to engage with the people who've been to your pop up.

Pages are visible to everyone, even those who haven't signed up to use Facebook, so they can help increase the reach of your pop up. Facebook users who've clicked the Like button to follow your Page's updates have started a relationship, and you can easily keep in touch with them.

Offering prizes, discounts or exclusive products to your Facebook fans increases both the sign-up rate and the degree of engagement with your pop up.

Flickr groups

A Flickr group is another way to create engagement with visitors. Create a group and encourage members to add their photos to it. Consider using incentives, such as a prize for the best photo, to get more people adding pictures.

Part V
Looking to the Future

The 5th Wave   By Rich Tennant

"Business here is good, but the weak dollar is killing my overseas markets!"

In this part . . .

*P*op ups are, by their very nature, as transient as blossoms in spring or a passing smile. That, of course, is what makes them special. But your business is more permanent; it's there before the pop up, and will (hopefully) be around after it – probably getting ready for another pop up, in fact!

In this part, I talk about how to make sure your pop up is embedded as part of your bigger business, through documenting what you do, evaluating what works and feeding that into plans for the future. I also look at how you can sustain the relationships you make during your pop up, leading to great things in the future.

Chapter 13

Measuring the Success of Your Pop Up

'*B*egin with the end in mind,' says Stephen Covey in his book *The 7 Habits of Highly Effective People* (Simon & Schuster Ltd). It's a very good point, as you really do need to know what your pop up will do before you start. Opening a pop up without some idea of what the impact will be, and how you'll measure whether it's a success or not, is a bit pointless.

You also need to remember what the point of a pop up is and that it will pop down, too. Don't be disappointed when you have to close. Carrying out an evaluation can help you decide whether to do another pop up and how to make sure that, if you do, you'll do it even better.

Evaluating Leads to Improvement

Evaluation is something you do every day in your normal life. If you plant bulbs in the garden, your measure of success is flowers growing. If you buy tickets to the cinema, your measure is a sense of enjoyment. If you don't achieve your desired results, the next time you buy different bulbs that suit your soil or avoid romantic comedies in the future and stick to sci-fi.

Evaluation is about looking at what worked and what didn't. When you evaluate your success, you look at some very specific, measurable attainments and at some more subjective measures of satisfaction as well.

Evaluation is not about *proving* what you've done to somebody else, but about working things out and *improving* what you do, for yourself.

And evaluation's not something that's done to you; it's part of your own learning and development.

For evaluation to be effective, you need three things:

- ✔ **Evidence** of what's happened, including information about numbers (*quantitative* data) and information about people's experiences (*qualitative* data).

- ✔ **Thinking** about the evidence, your pop up, how it worked and the experience your visitors had.

- ✔ **Learning** what can help you improve your business, the product and service you deliver in future.

Evaluation can seem like a chore, particularly when it comes immediately after a busy period of planning and then putting your pop up on show.

Evaluation is always worth doing, though, because it:

- ✔ Makes you more confident in your work.

- ✔ Informs your future plans.

- ✔ Focuses you on your customers.

- ✔ Motivates your staff and your partners.

- ✔ Encourages fundraisers and partners to support future work.

Looking at Your Measures of Success

What does success look like? It may be achieving a high volume of sales or just one or two really important ones. It may be attracting thousands of visitors or just ten. It may have nothing to do with numbers. Or perhaps success is simply a good experience for visitors or new skills learned by your team. How you measure success is very much tailored to your pop up.

You can measure success in many ways. Consider six main areas:

- Aim
- Timetable
- Budget and sales
- Team satisfaction
- Customer experience and visitor numbers
- Quality and honest mistakes

Aim

Did you achieve the aim you set yourself right at the start? (See Chapter 2 for more on setting aims.) You may have set out to:

- Hold a seasonal sale or event.
- Test or prototype a new business, product, range or service.
- Carry out market research for a new product, range or service.
- Launch a new product.
- Reach a different audience than your usual one.
- Take your business to a different place than the one where you usually do it.
- Stage a special event to increase customer loyalty or introduce new customers to your brand.

At the end of your pop up, you can judge whether you fulfilled your original aim. (Your aim is separate from your objectives, and Chapter 2 explains why.) Be honest and don't worry if you didn't achieve everything you set out to do. Use your evaluation to inform future work and try again.

Timetable

Your plan had set objectives, which were measurable and mapped to a timetable. You can easily reference these objectives to see whether you achieved everything you set out to do and whether you worked to the timetable you set yourself.

Record what worked well and what you'd like to do the same next time.

If some of the items on your timetable slipped, you must have picked them up again if you opened your pop up on time. Look at whether:

- ✔ Your original timetable was reasonable.
- ✔ You could have changed the order of actions to make the project easier.
- ✔ You included unnecessary things in your plan and timetable.

If you included things in your original timetable that turned out to be unnecessary, check your evaluation to see whether it was because of the way things turned out or whether they were things that simply weren't needed.

Look closely at whether additional resources, such as more support or the right equipment, would have made your timetable easier.

Budget and sales

At the end of your pop up, you can see where the money was spent. Look at all the costs you incurred:

- ✔ Materials, from paint and brushes to toilet paper and black sacks.

- ✔ Furniture, fixtures and fittings.

- ✔ Printed publicity and distribution costs, such as leaflets, posters and business cards.

- ✔ Signs, window vinyls and graphics, and an A-board.

- ✔ Website and Internet costs.

- ✔ Media advertising.

- ✔ Business rates.

- ✔ Utility bills.

- ✔ Insurance coverage.

- ✔ Refreshments (day to day and at opening events).

- ✔ Phone and broadband.

All of the preceding costs combined make up your project's expenditure. Now, look at all the income generated:

- ✔ Funding or budget found within an organisation.

- ✔ Donations from the public.

- ✔ Contributions to the project, such as from artists paying to hang work.

- ✔ Sponsorship or cash donations.

- ✔ Grant funding from local authorities, Arts Council England or trusts and foundations.

If your income was greater than your expenditure, you're *in profit*.

If your expenditure is equal to or less than you anticipated when you set your budget, you're also *within budget*.

A cash profit may not have been the aim of your pop up. If you were looking to test an idea, launch a project, engage with the community or build a better relationship with customers, don't count a cash loss as the failure of the pop up.

Pop up trains young people

Working with a team of artists, participants in the Culture Quarter Programme opened a pop up in the Seven Dials area of London. Seven Days in Seven Dials was produced entirely in a week working in a shop and then opened to visitors for two weeks. The pop up created an alternative tourist guide to the area, supporting local businesses and the Seven Dials area as a whole.

Working together, 30 young people researched, scripted and produced an audio tour, available as a podcast. They made a series of short films, exploring the seven streets that lead off of Seven Dials. And they held an exhibition exploring the creative and cultural history of the area. The videos received many views, the podcast was downloaded hundreds of times and more than 500 people visited the exhibition.

While those outcomes were successful in their own right, they weren't the principal reason for running the pop up. The Culture Quarter Programme was a scheme placing over 100 young people who had been unemployed in paid work experience placements in London's leading cultural organisations. The Royal Opera House, National Portrait Gallery, Design Council, English National Opera and other major organisations all participated, hosting placements for six months.

To ensure that the young people involved were given support and mentoring to develop real skills, they took part in a programme of workshops and seminars. They also developed their own cultural events. The Seven Days in Seven Dials was the most ambitious of these events.

While the programme was successful as a pop up in its own right, the real success was in the way it brought young people together, developing their teamwork, leadership and creative skills.

Team satisfaction

The positive benefits to the team involved in a pop up are often overlooked.

Many companies happily spend money sending their team to build rafts, swing from trees or bundle down the sides of mountains on quad bikes.

Team-building helps people:

- ✔ Develop stronger relationships.
- ✔ Share a positive experience.
- ✔ Identify skills and talents.
- ✔ Improve problem-solving skills.

Being involved in designing, building and managing a pop up achieves many of these goals as well, while delivering more benefits to the business than just getting cold and muddy.

Include examples of how the pop up has helped team members in these areas in your evaluation.

Customer experience and visitor numbers

In evaluating your customer's experience, you can look at:

- ✔ Visitor numbers
- ✔ Dwell time
- ✔ Conversion rates (measuring *either* sales or engagement)

For more information on conversion rates, see Chapter 12.

This quantitative data is useful, but it only gives you some of the information about the experience your customers had.

If you used a visitors' book or some other interactive way for people to comment (such as sticky notes on a sign), you can include some comments from visitors, adding a qualitative analysis.

Online impact

Your website, email lists and social media channels can provide further evidence for evaluation.

Again, you can provide quantitative data, such as:

- ✓ Visits to your website
- ✓ Followers on Twitter
- ✓ Friends on Facebook

You can increase your analysis by using sites that measure influence and impact. Although using and understanding them can take some time, these sites are some of the most useful:

- ✓ www.tweetreach.com is a simple tool for seeing just how far a tweet or hashtag has gone, giving you a snapshot of how many people have seen them. You can measure *all* tweets with your hashtag, which is very useful!

- ✓ www.klout.com measures the influence of your principal social media accounts based on your ability to drive action on social media.

- ✓ www.kred.com goes a little further than Klout, by allowing you to factor in achievements in the real world, such as memberships of other organisations.

- ✓ www.twentyfeet.com also tracks and measures your social media use, providing easy-to-understand facts and figures.

In addition to this quantitative data, look through Facebook Pages, hashtags and so on for more qualitative data. Status updates, tweets and comments reveal how people feel about your pop up, what they liked or didn't like and other experience-based evidence.

Quality and honest mistakes

Perhaps the hardest judgement to make is about the quality of your pop up. Quality is an entirely subjective analysis, but you can base it on comparisons with other business, events or activities within your market sector. This measurement relies on your knowledge and experience of your area.

Think about the:

- Branding, design and visual merchandising.
- Quality of products or services.
- Experience for customers.

Creative people (and the best entrepreneurs are really creative) know that failure is important, particularly when you're prototyping and testing new ideas and different ways of working. If you fail fast, which pop ups let you do, you can quickly carry on. By making mistakes, you learn and do better next time.

Don't be ashamed to admit that not everything about your pop up worked. Where you identify mistakes:

- Be honest about what went wrong.
- Identify fixes for next time.
- Don't apportion blame to an individual.

Measuring the Success of Your Partnerships

If you're working with a range of partners (see Chapter 3), those partners may have wanted you to collect and share certain data. Your agreements with them would have set out this expectation.

For example, a funding agreement states clearly what evaluation you have to provide. Usually, full and final funds are released only after this evaluation occurs.

Ideally, your partners will want to be involved in helping you to evaluate the pop up. It's in their interests to have some measure of your success, whether they're a self-employed artist or a government-funded organisation.

Hands-on partners

The partners who've been involved in the day-to-day running of your pop up probably have a clear and, more important, measurable idea of how they see success. Depending on how they were involved, it may be based on the:

- Amount of sales.
- Number of people met.
- Quantity of leaflets given out.

Your partners will have a good understanding of how the pop up worked and what it delivered.

Volunteers

Speak to more than one person who's volunteered, and you'll get more than one reason why they did it! Ask why people have volunteered because it may help you identify good things to offer volunteers in future projects.

Some of the likely benefits of volunteering are to:

- Give something back to the community.
- Enhance employability skills.
- Boost confidence.
- Learn something new.
- Have fun!

Strategic partners

People who've become more strategic partners in your pop up will have done so because your work overlaps in some way with theirs. They may be working in areas such as:

- Tourism.
- Economic development.
- Education and training.

✔ Voluntary and community sector development.

✔ Arts or culture.

When drawing up any agreement to work with such partners, they should have been very clear about what they expected, and consequently it should be easy to measure whether you've achieved that goal.

Do ask your strategic partners to provide evaluations. If your partner is a larger organisation, it may well produce such work internally in any case.

Their measures of success may be about the quality of the experience or about indirect benefits. Strategic partners may not be looking for evidence of sales or high visitor numbers, but may be interested in whether your pop up:

✔ Led to engagement with visitors.

✔ Increased their brand awareness.

✔ Encouraged debate around an issue.

✔ Contributed to a wider strategic target.

✔ Generated leads or new contacts.

✔ Provided evidence to inform future work.

Stakeholders

Some people you chose not to form strategic partnerships with may also be interested in measuring the success of your pop up and evaluating the work you've done. (For more about the difference between strategic partners and stakeholders, see Chapter 3.)

If your pop up has had an effect on their work, you may find your pop up referenced in their plans, strategies and even more casually in their blogs and newsletters.

Watch out for any evidence about your pop up from stakeholders, as this may be useful to inform your future work and to build future partnerships.

Writing Your Evaluation

Your evaluation needs to talk to an audience both inside your business sector and to possible partners outside as well.

As you write your evaluation, keep the following pointers in mind:

- Avoid using jargon, slang and technical terms.
- Use simple English.
- Be clear.
- Excite people.
- Keep it brief.

Your evaluation will include many voices, from your team and your customers. But it's best if one person leads on the writing, asking experts to comment on and inform the evaluation as needed.

Ensure your evaluation is honest. Pop ups are often about prototyping and testing, and because of that, failure is a perfectly acceptable outcome! When evaluating your pop up, do look at what mistakes happened and why, but do not blame somebody – that's not the point of evaluation.

Don't spend more time evaluating your pop up than you did running it. Evaluation should take no more than 10 per cent of the total time and resources dedicated to your pop up.

Be careful about possible privacy issues when writing your evaluation. Remove names from any comments so that they're anonymous. Be careful when naming any members of your team, too. If you want to include names, ensure that you comply with local data protection and privacy laws. You may need to ask people you quote for permission to use their comments, or display a sign by your visitor book or comment wall explaining that some quotes will be used in your evaluation.

Sharing Evaluation

Your evaluation is a valuable record of the work you've done, and this is true whether your pop up exceeded all your expectations or fizzled like a soggy firework.

Making a summary or even all of your evaluation available online is worth doing because it:

- ✔ Widens the audience for your pop up.
- ✔ Demonstrates your skills and capabilities.
- ✔ Attracts interest and enquiries.
- ✔ Can be used by media looking for stories about pop ups or, more specifically, your business sector.

After you've made some evaluation available, use your social media channels to share it. People who visited your pop up will almost certainly want to see it and to share it with their networks.

Consider creating an evaluation in a form that's more interesting than a written report – for example, as an infographic or a short film. Such content can easily go viral and ensure that your pop up lives long after you've closed the doors.

You don't have to wait until closing day to begin your evaluation. Take a few minutes out at the end of each day to discuss performance with your staff, or to reflect on results if you're working alone. You can use the daily objectives highlighted in the preceding chapter as your agenda.

Chapter 14

Packing Up and Moving On

*P*art of the philosophy of a pop up is that you'll be packing up and moving on soon. That's what sets a pop up apart from other shops.

After you achieve the results you planned and review them, your team disbands. You move on to the next project or return to your everyday work.

If you're not mentally prepared for this process, you can do some real damage. Your customers may feel that they've been let down by your leaving. And your team won't be able to learn from the experience, have a sense that a job's well done, and move on to what's next either. Worst of all, you may feel like you haven't finished the work you started and feel frustrated, too.

In this chapter, I show you how to close down your pop up after you've carried out your evaluation (see Chapter 13). I also look at how to make sure that your experience and your evaluation can help you move onto new projects.

I talk about the 'project' rather than 'pop up' in this chapter because some of the things I discuss take place *after* your actual pop up space has closed.

Saying Goodbye to the Shop

The date your pop up will close isn't a secret. Your lease ends on a set date, you've achieved your aims and you have nothing left to do except the evaluation (see Chapter 13). You've done all the work you set out to do.

Your closing process needs to be part of your planning from the very start so that you have the resources and all the information you need to make closing a smooth operation.

Sometimes, pop ups can feel like they've become permanent – for example, if a group of artists occupy space on a rolling month-to-month licence. In this case, you must be clear that your shop is still a pop up, and everybody who's involved must be made aware that you could leave at short notice.

You need to have a closure plan in place and communicate it to everyone who uses the space. You must either accept the decision to close when circumstances outside your control make it happen, or be clear about what will trigger your own decision to close your pop up.

Use this checklist to help:

- ✔ The date for closing the pop up is confirmed.

- ✔ The process for evaluating the project is in place, and it's agreed how that evaluation will be prepared and shared.

- ✔ All staff and team members are aware of the date the pop up closes and know what happens next.

- ✔ Any staff on temporary contracts know when they'll end.

- ✔ Any assets, such as remaining stock, fixtures and fittings, and intellectual property, such as logos, are assigned to a new home.

- ✔ Follow-up actions are defined and assigned to team members.

The team who has made it all happen has worked hard. It's worth throwing some kind of celebration right at the end, possibly to present your evaluation but also to thank everyone who helped. Seeing what the pop up achieved can be a great boost and may help you keep people interested as you plan your next pop up.

Coming to an Emergency Stop

Sometimes your pop up comes to an emergency stop, usually because of a change of circumstance that's outside your control.

Don't panic; closing early is quite common. An early closing may occur because of a lack of funding or funding allocations change. Or perhaps the building is let unexpectedly to a long-term tenant, or an unexpected issue, such as a problem with the building's structure, occurs.

If you come to an emergency stop, you usually have two options:

- ✔ Close the project early.
- ✔ Find alternative premises.

If you've planned your pop up in an agile way (see Chapter 2), you'll be able to adapt to new premises. In this case:

1. **Stop for as long as you need.**

2. **Communicate to partners (and maybe to customers) that you've stopped.**

3. **Identify how to carry on.**

    For example, can you find alternative premises or different funding?

4. **Check that these revisions still allow you to achieve your original aims and objectives and revise them, if needed.**

5. **Revise your timetable to reflect the change.**

6. **Keep calm and carry on!**

If you do decide to finish early, you:

- ✔ Still need to close the project properly, tidying up loose ends and carrying out evaluation of work done.

- ✔ Must salvage anything that you can use and make sure that it's ready for future use. (See the upcoming 'Dealing with assets' section.)

- ✔ Need to tell stakeholders that you've stopped and why and obtain their agreement, if necessary.

- ✔ Must communicate with your audience so that it's not disappointed.

Tidying Up Loose Ends

With lots of partners, different people sharing and using your space and all sorts of activity going on, you have many loose ends to tie up before you can take your shoes off and sit down with a good cup of tea.

It's not over until the fat lady has sung, packed up the stage set, tidied up behind herself, said goodbye to all the people she worked with and turned off the lights!

Cleaning your pop up venue

The space you used was absolutely essential to the success of your pop up. You got that space because you invested time in building a relationship with the owner. You don't want to damage that relationship right at the end. Even though you're tired and feel like it's all over, you still have one very important job to do. You need to get the space you used ready to hand back to its owner.

Always aim to hand the venue you used back to its owner in better condition than you got it. Make sure that you take the following steps:

✔ Remove everything you brought into the shop, except the things you'll need to clean up and redecorate.

✔ Take down your branding, including shop vinyls and any signs. You can remove vinyls from windows with a sharp blade and use window-cleaning products to remove any sticky marks.

✔ Repair any minor damage, including scuffed paintwork or holes you've made to fix things in place. Fill holes, sand and repaint. It's unlikely that you'll need to redecorate top to bottom, but do touch up paintwork with the colours you used to redecorate in the first place.

✔ Make sure that all light bulbs are working.

✔ Clear all rubbish. Any rubbish must be disposed of carefully and correctly. Your pop up is a commercial venture, as far as the authorities in charge of waste are concerned. You may be able to dispose of small amounts of day-to-day rubbish in your bins at home, but larger amounts of rubbish may incur costs.

Check with your local authority about how it deals with commercial waste. Try to reduce the amount of rubbish you generate by reusing and recycling as much as possible.

✔ Sweep floors, clean windows and scrub ancillary areas, such as toilets and kitchens. You won't make your shop spotless, but it needs to look clean and tidy, ready for the next user.

✔ Put anything that was found in the space when you were given the keys back where you found it.

After the space is clear, clean and tidy, arrange to meet the owner on site to return the keys. Make sure that the owner is happy with the condition of the space and make him aware of any improvements you've made to it.

Hopefully, he'll be happy with the work you've done and the way you used the shop. If so, you've still got a partner next time you want to pop up.

Dealing with assets

Throughout your pop up, you'll have made all sorts of things, from logos to leaflets and branding to banners. And you'll have gathered all sorts of useful things, too, from shopfittings to teaspoons.

When you close the project, you need to store everything you've made or used for future use or find it a new home, and return anything borrowed to its owner. Consider these details:

- **Furniture, fixtures and fittings** that are unwanted at the end of your pop up need a new home. A local charity shop, voluntary sector group or other organisation may be able to continue to use them. Otherwise, consider using your local Freegle, Freecycle or other recycling group to pass such items on.

- **Stock** left over can be stored for future use. Return any stock provided on a sale-or-return basis and check to ensure that all stock sold is accounted and paid for. Consider donating to charity anything that you won't need in the future or use your local Freegle or Freecycle group to pass on unwanted items.

- **Evaluation, documentation and branding** are valuable property, and somebody still needs to own them after your project has ended. Ownership won't be a problem if they're part of your brand, or you plan to continue the work your pop up started.

  But if not, consider whether you can pass these items on to a partner organisation. If you do, make sure that it's clear who takes responsibility for those assets in case they're needed in the future.

- **Websites and social media accounts** are valuable because they let you keep in touch with customers and contacts you've made. If you're continuing your work, make sure that they're maintained and updated.

  If not, consider whether to pass them to a partner or keep them dormant. If you hand them over, make it clear that this has happened by posting an update on your account's profile. If you decide to keep them dormant, make it clear with a message that says, 'This project ran from X to Y. For future work, contact Z'.

If you've borrowed anything and it's been lost or damaged, offer to make repairs or replace the item.

Handing over items

Whether you're working for yourself or delivering a pop up for somebody else, you need to make sure that everything's handed over to the right people at the end. Here are a few tips to make the handover a smooth process:

- ✔ Be clear from the start about who'll own what when your project is finished. Discuss this decision early in the project so that it doesn't cause arguments later on. You don't want a successful pop up to be spoilt by an argument over who owns what!

- ✔ When you do hand things over, be very clear about what's expected – for example, how they'll be made available to other people or used in future.

- ✔ Don't expect to retain control of things you've handed over; they now belong to somebody else who can do whatever they want with them.

Searching for the Next Big Thing

The end of a pop up is an interesting moment. On one hand, it's a relief that it's all over, and you can relax a little. But this feeling is always tempered with a sense of disappointment that it's all over and an urge to do it again. It's the same feeling that actors get when they come off stage every night.

Hopefully your sanity is intact, and so is your bank balance – in which case, it may be that the time is right to consider going out on the stage to perform again!

Pop ups exist to test and prototype ideas, so your pop up may be informing your future work. You may discover that, after you've refined an idea, you need another pop up to test that refinement.

Or it may be that, like a growing number of small producers, home-based traders, artists and makers or marketing departments in bigger brands, a pop up becomes a regular part of your work. You may open once or twice a year, and every time you do, you get a little bit better.

Gaining knowledge from pop ups

Evaluating your pop up is really important, which is why I devote a whole chapter to that topic (see Chapter 13). But don't think that producing an evaluation is the end. If you've done your evaluation in a way that's thorough, informative and useful, it means you're learning. That means that what happens next is informed by what's gone on before.

Evaluating your project and learning from that evaluation means that:

- ✔ You're more confident in your work.
- ✔ Your future plans and projects are better informed.
- ✔ You have an improved focus on your customers.
- ✔ Your team, including your staff and your partners, are more motivated.
- ✔ Fundraisers and future partners are more inclined to support your work.

For all of these benefits to happen, keep your evaluation close to hand, share it with people and refer to it as your work carries on.

Consider how sharing your evaluation may continue the work of your pop up. Consider depositing a copy with your local library, museum or local history archive so that it's publicly available and can help someone else in the process. At the very least, make your evaluation available online in some form.

Staying friends

In the short time that your pop up is open, you have a huge impact on the people you work with.

You bring together a team and help them build bonds and friendships and acquire new skills under pressure. You help them make independent decisions. You and your team are pushed, tested and tried, but still get to the point where the curtain rises and everything happens as it should.

You show your partners new ways of working and give experience of different ways of doing things. And they receive all the benefits of a better relationship with customers, too. Use your evaluation to remind partners that, even though the pop up is closed and the project's finished, a relationship has still been formed.

Always keep an eye open for future opportunities to work together. You can do much more together.

It's an old truism that good friendships are formed in adversity. Pop ups have the same effect. It's up to you to make sure that those relationships, both professional and personal, continue.

Part VI

The Part of Tens

In this part . . .

I end with the famous *For Dummies* Part of Tens, concise and information-packed lists of fun but useful tips.

In this part I give you ten essential items for your pop up, from a kettle to a stepladder, plus ten reasons why your pop up is good for business by fostering fun and making a difference to your community.

Chapter 15

Ten Useful Items to Have in Your Pop Up

*E*very pop up needs to have some things – and I'm not talking about the big things, such as an idea, great branding and so on. No, I'm talking about the smaller, more practical items that you can easily overlook.

The ten useful items I describe in this chapter can help you with the day-to-day running of your pop up. They tidy corners, soften edges and make the whole experience a little less stressful.

Coffee Machine or a Teapot

Ideally, have both a coffee machine and a teapot in your pop up. The presence of tea and coffee transforms your pop up. Your pop up instantly becomes more friendly and inviting, and your visitors feel more relaxed. Providing refreshments shows you're not a normal shop, but something new and more sociable.

Create a corner (even if it's out of public sight) where you can have the coffee machine on the go and boil a kettle. You don't need to become a cafe, but if your customers are really interested, offering them a tea or coffee while they make up their mind may just sway them.

Coffee and tea also stops you and your team flagging when the going feels hard. Make the tea and coffee corner the first thing you unpack when you get the keys and the last thing you pack away when you finish.

Tables

At times, you may need an extra work surface. For example, when you're setting up, running a workshop, holding a launch party or packing up, a couple of extra tables are useful.

Folding decorators' tables are ideal; unlike larger commercial trestle tables, they fold in half and fit into the boot of a normal car. Don't buy cheap wooden ones; they fall apart far too quickly. Professional painters and decorators use high-quality, metal-framed pasting tables, and the most stylish ones look really good and are firm and sturdy to work on.

Seats

Shopping is becoming far more social. A seating area in your pop up helps visitors feel more comfortable and increases the time they spend with you. A sofa is ideal, of course, although not always practical.

Have a few chairs around for people to take a breather or create a seating area with tables and chairs near your coffee machine.

Have a few folding or stacking seats as well, in case your pop up gets really busy.

Heaters (or a Fan)

Empty shops seem to be universally cold or far too hot. Electric fan heaters are fast and effective, but they do add to the electricity bill.

You know how shops always have a heater over the door? It creates a warm air curtain to stop cold air coming in – and it works. So put one heater near the door.

In summer, it's guaranteed your shop will be far too hot. An electric fan keeps the air moving and cools down the shop quickly.

Notice as well how often your customers' first comments are 'It's nice and warm in here' or 'It's good to find a cool spot'.

WiFi Access

No pop up is complete without WiFi access. Fortunately, a gadget called a MiFi connects to mobile broadband and then acts as a WiFi router for up to five laptops or other devices. A MiFi, which is the size of a mobile phone, is ideal for creating temporary WiFi hotspots in empty shops and provides a reliable, robust connection. It costs £50–100.

Using a MiFi enables you to work on a laptop from the shop and engage with your audience on social media.

Offer WiFi to visitors, and they'll stay longer, and you have more chance to engage them in what you're doing.

Bed Sheets

Using fabric softens a space, gets rid of nasty echoes and hides clutter. Single bed sheets are about the right size for covering trestle or pasting tables. They also make handy curtains, can be pulled tight to make fake walls and are useful for window displays.

Buy a load in one colour to match your branding, and your space looks co-ordinated.

Toolkit

You need a few tools, and with a useful toolkit, you should be able to pull off that Mary Poppins trick and look prepared for any emergency.

You don't need anything special: just a claw hammer, pliers, scissors, a couple of screwdrivers and a staple gun. Add gaffer tape, masking tape, nylon fishing wire, small tacks or nails, drawing pins and staples, and you're ready. Sticky tack, bulldog clips and dressmaking pins are also useful for displaying things.

Stepladder

At some point in every pop up you need to reach a little higher. You may need to clean windows, hang artwork, touch up paintwork or just place something on a shelf.

Balancing on chairs really isn't a good idea. Steps are. Ideally have a small set, just three steps high, for small jobs and a full-size stepladder ready for when you need it.

Broom

Empty shops and other spaces regularly used for pop ups are dusty. A good vacuum cleaner is useful, but a broom, dustpan and brush are more useful for day-to-day use. Keeping your shop clean really improves its look, and even the most interesting, gritty and urban spaces look better when the floor's swept.

In particularly dusty shops, a fine water spray, such as the type used for spraying plants or favoured by hairdressers, is very useful. Spraying lightly before you dust ensures you don't simply sweep the dust into the air and around the room.

Stacking Boxes

You have stock to organise, as well as day-to-day supplies, leaflets, cleaning supplies and a dozen other things. Without a little organisation, your pop up can start to look like it's popped apart.

Stacking boxes are invaluable for keeping your pop up tidy. The best sort are those plastic crates used by businesses to move office; they're heavy duty and have a lid, too.

Label boxes clearly so that everyone knows what belongs where. Don't write directly on the boxes, as labels may change; use strips of packing tape and remember to label at least two opposite sides so that whichever way the boxes are stacked, you know what's in them.

Chapter 16

Ten Reasons Why Your Pop Up Is Good for Business

*P*op ups are an incredibly useful tool for doing business; they're like a Swiss army penknife, which pops out in all sorts of useful ways. So what you do with your pop up is entirely up to you. The only limit is the edge of your imagination.

This book doesn't give you a template, but it can make starting a pop up easier and help you avoid mistakes.

In this chapter, I list ten common pop up themes.

Have a Message

Pop ups aren't just shops; they are, by their very nature, something special. They have a magical, ephemeral quality, like blossoms in spring, and they do something that other shops on the high street just don't do.

Whether your pop up is testing a new idea, giving something special to valued customers or has a social purpose, make sure that your message is clear. Use your decor, kit-out, marketing and social media to convey your message and tell the story behind your brand.

Be Local

Many people are living much more locally in the last few years. Social media has helped people form strong, local groups – global networks, for local action! And people are keen to 'Shop Local', too.

The best pop ups are celebrating the local by discovering what's distinctive about the place where they happen and exciting the neighbourhood. Make your pop up relevant to the place where it happens and the people who live nearby. Not only will you find your pop up more rewarding, it will be easier too, as local networks mobilise to support your work.

Do Something Different

Are you bored of the nine to five grind? Find yourself doing the same things, week in, week out?

Pop ups exist so that you can break out of the routine, be creative and do things differently. They're still part of your core business, especially if you get your aims right in the first place and stick to them throughout the time you're planning and running your pop up (see Chapter 2 for more on aims).

But pop ups are about innovation and give you the perfect chance to test and prototype new products and services. The risks aren't as great as they would be if you took a long-term lease. You can be in and out in a matter of weeks, from the day you start planning to the day you get back to normal.

So take a chance; use a pop up to do something different.

Change the Rules

Pop ups, even the most corporate ones, have a mischievous, slightly anarchic spirit. They're about finding new uses for old spaces, being temporary not permanent and trying new things. They're not about doing things the way they've already been done.

You don't have to be dangerous; this book covers risk assessment (Chapter 2), finance (Chapter 4) and leases, licences and the legal stuff (Chapter 5). (I did say only *slightly* anarchic!) But pop ups do give you a chance to build new teams, push the boundaries and bend things to meet your aim.

It's time to rewrite the rulebook.

Be a Coffee Shop

The prototype Next store in Shoreham by Sea sells clothes and furniture and has a Starbucks cafe. The Orange community shop in Monmouth is used as a community shop but still sells mobile phones. The Rough Trade record store in London's Brick Lane is a cafe, bookshop and occasional venue.

Some people predict that, in the future, everything will be a coffee shop that does something else as well.

What they really mean is that the social element of shopping will become more important. Add a coffee machine, stock up on biscuits and make cups of tea for your customers; you create a more friendly pop up and keep customers engaged for longer. (For additional ways to make your pop up more inviting, see Chapter 10.)

Don't Hang Around

In the past 50 years, people have assumed that permanent equals important, that being old gives you authority and that the established equals the powerful. But the world is accelerating.

Things that exist for a short time add interest and meaning to places. Think about the number of events you go to that pop up; farmers' markets, craft fairs, street performers and music festivals all bring life and vibrancy to the places where they happen. And nobody thinks of their website as a permanent, set in stone, unchanging thing.

Be proud to be a pop up and be agile (see Chapter 2 for more on this concept). Don't try to be permanent!

Learn from Failure

In today's culture, success is all that matters. Creative people know, though, that failure is more important; by making mistakes, you learn and do better next time. As playwright Samuel Becket said, 'Try again. Fail again. Fail better.'

Entrepreneurs know that failure fosters success, too. Virgin Brides, Virgin Cosmetics, Virgin Megastores and Virgin Cola weren't successes, but they all helped Sir Richard Branson become one of the richest people in Britain.

Pop ups are a perfect place to test and prototype, but it means some ideas will fail. Don't be scared to fail, but do reap the lessons when you do. Fail faster!

Recycle Empty Shops

Pop ups recycle old shops, old furniture and shop fittings, and many even sell recycled and remade goods, too.

Creating new things from old is common to lots of pop ups. Think of your pop up as part of the cycle of life on the high street. Make sure that you reduce, reuse and recycle. Whatever's left at the end of your pop up, pass on and share.

Come Together

Get people together to make your pop up work. Working with a group is more fun than working alone, so find people you can trust and let them do what they're best at. Don't micro-manage.

Pop ups are often shared spaces, with loose partnerships delivering mixed programmes of activity in their shops. Chapter 3 tells you how to build a team and form partnerships. Round up a posse, and you'll find that, as singer Sufjan Stevens says. 'We can do much more together – it's not so impossible'.

Have Fun

Whether your pop up flies or crashes into the ground, it's an unusual chance to try things out. You work with a great, hand-picked team of people to achieve a common aim. You get a chance to be creative. You meet interesting visitors, too; pop ups do attract the local characters!

So make sure, amongst all the planning, the push to open on time and under the pressure of delivering, to have fun.

That's why people like me become pop up addicts; because it's just about the most fun you can have on the high street.

Index

Notes

About the Author

Dan Thompson is an artist and writer based in an insignificant town on the south coast of England. He's a recognised expert on the reuse of empty shops, and on how to create a pop up shop.

In 2000, Dan founded Revolutionary Arts, and started using empty shops for arts and community projects. Since then, he has provided advice and support to projects across the UK, and spoken at workshops, festivals and seminars across the country and in Holland. He has worked for Unilever, RIBA, Place NI, vInspired, University of the Arts, Spacemakers, Yell and others. Before writing *Pop Up Business For Dummies*, Dan wrote the *Empty Shops Toolkit* for the Government's Living Places programme. In 2012, he authored and published *Pop Up People*, the first study of pop up culture, which has been read by government ministers. TV star Mary Portas referenced his work in her *High Street Review* for the British Government.

Dan has written about the problems facing town centres for *The Independent* and *The Guardian*. Other media includes *The Sunday Times*, *Evening Standard* and *The Stylist*, and he has also featured in news reports on BBC News, Radio 4, Sky News, ABC and CNN.

After the riots across England in 2011, Dan started #riotcleanup, using Twitter to galvanise thousands of people to take action in their local community. For this, he was singled out by David Cameron as an example of great British leadership. Dan has since built www.wewillgather.co.uk, a project inspired by #riotcleanup and funded by Nesta and the Government's Office for Civil Society.

Dan made *The Independent* Happy List 2012, the BBC Radio 4 iPM Alternative New Year Honours 2011, received a Team London Award from the Mayor of London, was named in GQ's 100 Most Influential list and was winner of the Coast Awards 2011 'Unsung Hero' trophy.

Dedication

To my parents, Netta and Nigel, for being supportive over many years of my oddball career; and to their parents Betty and Geoff, Edie and Jack for being inspirational.

To my wife Tracey and children Dayna, Edward and Eliza, primarily for supporting me while I criss-cross the country working on crazed plans and half-baked schemes, but especially for letting me lock myself in the back room at home to write this book in a few weeks in 2012.

Author's Acknowledgments

This book wouldn't have happened without all the people who've filled empty shops with their interesting ideas. You're changing the world, one shop at a time.

The ideas in this book come from working with many people on Revolutionary Arts projects, and special thanks to everybody who has commissioned that organisation to deliver projects, supported its work, taken part in exhibitions and events, and most importantly been the Revolutionary Arts audience.

Many thanks to Claire Ruston, Rachael Chilvers and all at Wiley for their help and advice in writing this book.

Publisher's Acknowledgments

We're proud of this book; please send us your comments at http://dummies. custhelp.com. For other comments, please contact our Customer Care Department within the U.S. at 877-762-2974, outside the U.S. at (001) 317-572-3993, or fax 317-572-4002.

Some of the people who helped bring this book to market include the following:

Acquisitions, Editorial, and Vertical Websites

Commissioning Editor: Claire Ruston

Project Editor: Rachael Chilvers

Assistant Editor: Ben Kemble

Development Editor: Kelly Ewing

Technical Editor: Colin Barrow

Proofreader: Kate O'Leary

Production Manager: Daniel Mersey

Publisher: David Palmer

Cover Photo: © Marco Rosario Venturini Autieri / iStock

Cartoons: Rich Tennant (www.the5thwave.com)

Composition Services

Senior Project Coordinator: Kristie Rees

Layout and Graphics: Jennifer Creasey

Proofreader: Melanie Hoffman

Indexer: Claudia Bourbeau

FOR DUMMIES®

Making Everything Easier! ™

UK editions

BUSINESS

Bookkeeping
978-0-470-97626-5

Persuasion & Influence
978-0-470-74737-7

Starting & Running a Business
978-1-119-97527-4

REFERENCE

British Politics
978-0-470-68637-9

DIY
978-0-470-97450-6

Dad's Guide to Pregnancy
978-1-119-97660-8

HOBBIES

Growing Your Own Fruit & Veg
978-0-470-69960-7

Keeping Chickens
978-1-119-99417-6

Beekeeping
978-1-119-97250-1

Asperger's Syndrome For Dummies
978-0-470-66087-4

Basic Maths For Dummies
978-1-119-97452-9

Body Language For Dummies, 2nd Edition
978-1-119-95351-7

Boosting Self-Esteem For Dummies
978-0-470-74193-1

British Sign Language For Dummies
978-0-470-69477-0

Cricket For Dummies
978-0-470-03454-5

Diabetes For Dummies, 3rd Edition
978-0-470-97711-8

Electronics For Dummies
978-0-470-68178-7

English Grammar For Dummies
978-0-470-05752-0

Flirting For Dummies
978-0-470-74259-4

IBS For Dummies
978-0-470-51737-6

Improving Your Relationship For Dummies
978-0-470-68472-6

ITIL For Dummies
978-1-119-95013-4

Management For Dummies, 2nd Edition
978-0-470-97769-9

Neuro-linguistic Programming For Dummies, 2nd Edition
978-0-470-66543-5

Nutrition For Dummies, 2nd Edition
978-0-470-97276-2

Organic Gardening For Dummies
978-1-119-97706-3

FOR DUMMIES®

Making Everything Easier! ™

UK editions

SELF-HELP

STUDENTS

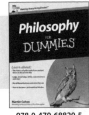

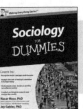

HISTORY

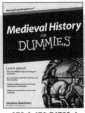

12–43522

FOR DUMMIES

Making Everything Easier!™

COMPUTER BASICS

978-0-470-57829-2

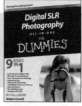

978-0-470-61454-9

978-0-470-49743-2

DIGITAL PHOTOGRAPHY

978-0-470-25074-7

978-0-470-76878-5

978-1-118-00472-2

MICROSOFT OFFICE 2010

978-0-470-48998-7

978-0-470-58302-9

978-0-470-48953-6

Access 2010 For Dummies
978-0-470-49747-0

Android Application Development
For Dummies
978-0-470-77018-4

AutoCAD 2011 For Dummies
978-0-470-59539-8

C++ For Dummies, 6th Edition
978-0-470-31726-6

Computers For Seniors
For Dummies, 2nd Edition
978-0-470-53483-0

Dreamweaver CS5 For Dummies
978-0-470-61076-3

iPad 2 For Dummies, 3rd Edition
978-1-118-17679-5

Macs For Dummies, 11th Edition
978-0-470-87868-2

Mac OS X Snow Leopard
For Dummies
978-0-470-43543-4

Photoshop CS5 For Dummies
978-0-470-61078-7

Photoshop Elements 10
For Dummies
978-1-118-10742-3

Search Engine Optimization
For Dummies, 4th Edition
978-0-470-88104-0

The Internet For Dummies,
13th Edition
978-1-118-09614-7

Visual Studio 2010 All-In-One
For Dummies
978-0-470-53943-9

Web Analytics For Dummies
978-0-470-09824-0

Word 2010 For Dummies
978-0-470-48772-3

WordPress For Dummies,
4th Edition
978-1-118-07342-1